THE SAINT OF BLEECKER STREET

MUSICAL DRAMA

in

THREE ACTS

(Five Scenes)

Words and Music by

Gian-Carlo Menotti

STAGE MATERIAL

With English and German Text

Ed. 2178

G. SCHIRMER, *Inc.*

7777 W. Bluemound Rd. P.O. Box 13819 Milwaukee, WI 53213

Note

A complete recording of The Saint of Bleecker Street has been issued on Long Playing Record by R.C.A. Victor.

"THE SAINT OF BLEECKER STREET", produced by Chandler Cowles, had its world première on December 27, 1954, at the Broadway Theatre in New York. The following cast took part in its performance:

Assunta	CATHERINE AKOS
Carmela	MARIA DI GERLANDO
Maria Corona	MARIA MARLO
Her dumb son	ERNESTO GONZALES
Don Marco	LEON LISHNER
Annina	VIRGINIA COPELAND
Michele	DAVID POLERI
Desideria	GLORIA LANE
Salvatore	DAVID AIKEN
Concettina	LUCY BECQUE
A young man	RICHARD CASSELLI
An old woman	ELIZABETH CARRON
Bartender	RUSSELL GOODWIN
First guest	KEITH KALDENBERG
Second guest	JACK REARDON
A nun	DOROTHY KREBILL
A young priest	ROBERT BARRY

The entire production was staged by Mr. Menotti.
The orchestra was directed by Thomas Schippers.

The Saint of Bleecker Street

Act One

Scene I

German Translation by
Karlheinz Gutheim and Wilhelm Reinking

Words and Music by
Gian-Carlo Menotti

(A cold-water flat in the tenements of Bleecker Street. Upstage, the entrance from the hallway. Stage right, a door leading to Annina's bedroom. Next to it a small, heavily adorned altar displaying a monochrome picture of the Virgin. Stage left, a kitchen stove and an iron bed. As the curtain opens, a group of neighbors, some standing, some kneeling, are grouped around Assunta, who is chanting the Litany. They are all facing the half-open door of Annina's room.)

2
sempre f
ff
p
3
pp

4
Curtain
attacca
5
Lento, ma non troppo
Assunta
A'ta
Ro - sa My - sti - ca,
tur - ris da - vi - di - ca,
SOPRANO
O - ra pro no - bis,
o - ra pro no - bis,
ALTO
TENOR
Chorus
O - ra pro no - bis,
o - ra pro no - bis,
BASS
Lento, ma non troppo

A'ta
tur-ris e bur - ne-a,
do-mus au - re - a,
o - ra pro no-bis,
o - ra pro no-bis,
o - ra pro no-bis,
o - ra pro no-bis,
A'ta
foe - de-ris ar - ca,
ja - nua coe - li,
o - ra pro no-bis,
o - ra pro no-bis,
o - ra pro no-bis,
o - ra pro no-bis,

A'ta
stel - la ma-tu-ti - na,
sa - lus in-fir-mo-rum,
re -
o - ra pro no-bis,
o - ra pro no-bis.
o - ra pro no-bis,
o - ra pro no-bis
A'ta
fu-gium pec-ca-to...
A young man tiptoes to the bedroom door and peeks through.
sh! Pst!
6
Allegro
Allegro
p

Why don't they bring her out?
Wann bringt man sie her-aus?
What do you see?
Kannst du was sehn?
What do you see?
Kannst du was sehn?
Why don't they bring her out?
A young man
She moves, she weeps.
Sie bewegt sich, sie weint.
We wait - ed long e - nough.
Wir war - ten lang ge - nug.
We wait - ed long e - nough.
We wait - ed long e - nough.
We wait - ed long e - nough.

7
Young Man
They hold her down, they wipe her cheeks
Man hält sie fest, wischt ihr die Trä-nen ab.
She moves, she weeps.
Sie be-wegt sich, sie weint.
They wipe her cheeks.
Man wischt ihr die Tränen ab.
She moves, she weeps.
They wipe her cheeks
Young Man
They have moved her to her chair. Her eyes are glass-y like the
Man trägt sie in ih-ren Stuhl. Ih-re Au - gen sind starr, als wär' sie

Young Man
dead.
tot.
Watch out, watch out. They'll see you. Run
Pass auf, pass auf, man sieht dich. Komm
Watch out, watch out. They'll see you.
Pass auf, pass auf, man sieht dich.
Watch out, watch out. They'll see you.
Watch out, watch out. They'll see you. Run
f
8
Young Man
back.
her.
Bet-ter close the door!
Geh von der Tü - re weg!
Run back.
Komm her.
Run back.
Bet-ter close the door!
back.

Young Man
She moans, — she cries,
Sie stöhnt, — sie schreit,
She moans, she
Sie stöhnt, sie
She moans, she
Young Man
as if in great con - sum - ing pain.
als ob sie gros - se Schmer-zen hät - te.
cries,
schreit,
as if in
als hätt' sie
cries,
as if in

Young Man
9
I be-lieve her vi-sions have be - gun.
's ist so weit, die Vi - sio - nen fan - gen an.
pain.
Schmer-zen.
pain.
cresc.
Her vi-sions have be - gun. Why don't they bring her out?
Die Vi-sio-nen fan - gen an. Wann bringt man sie her - aus?
f

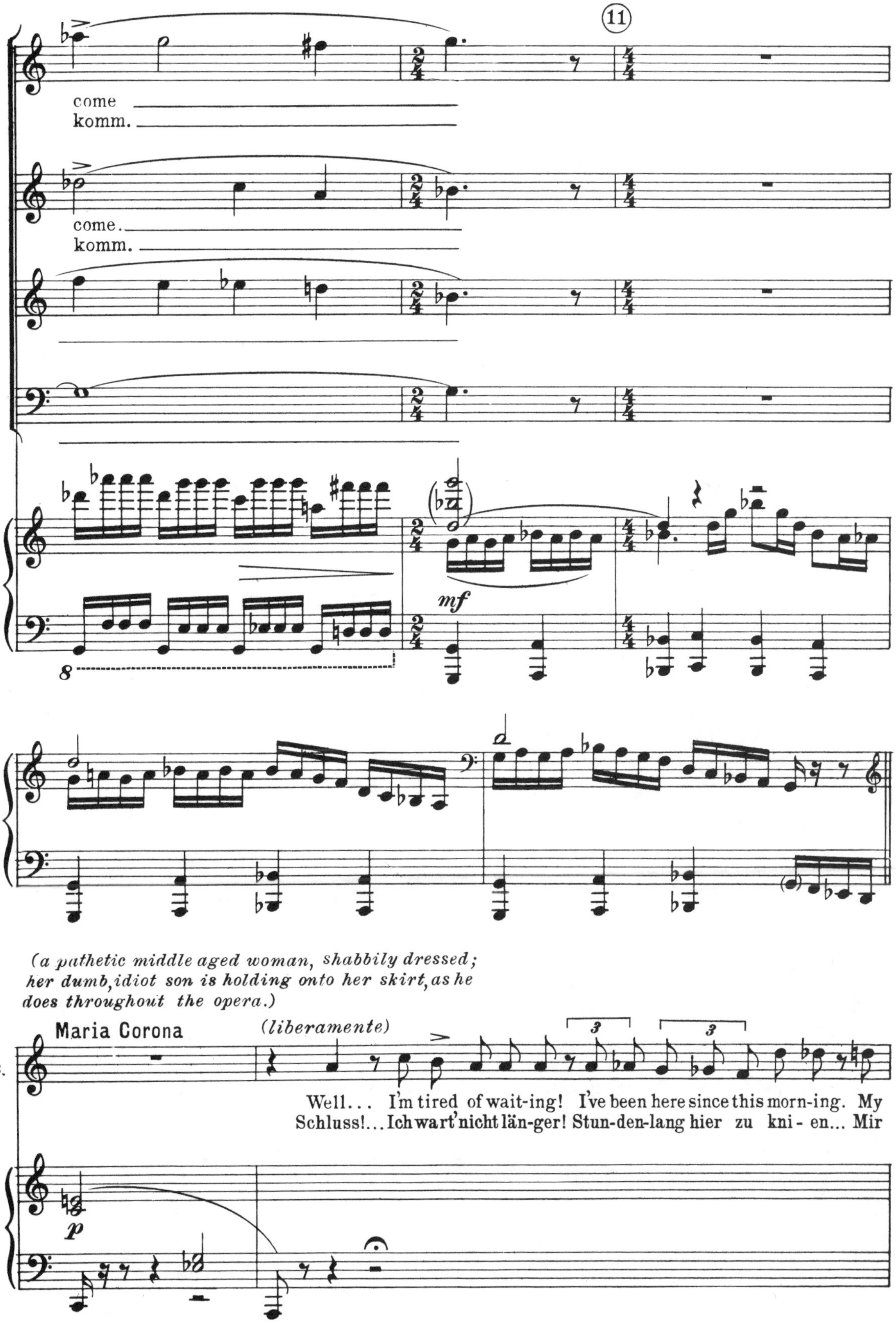

(11)

come
komm.

come.
komm.

mf

8

(a pathetic middle aged woman, shabbily dressed; her dumb, idiot son is holding onto her skirt, as he does throughout the opera.)

Maria Corona
12
M.C.
knees hurt.
langt's jetzt.
Assunta
A'ta
Don't be a fool.
Sei doch nicht dumm.
They'll bring her out an-y min-ute.
Sie wer-den sich-er bald kom-men.
pp
Maria Corona
M.C.
My poor child has had noth-ing to eat all day Be-
Mein Kind hat noch gar nichts zu es-sen ge-kriegt. Und
Poco meno mosso
p
M.C.
sides, who can prom-ise that my child will be cured?
wer ga-ran-tier, dass er ge-heilt wer-den wird?
One al-ways
Ja... ja, ge-

M.C.
3
hears a-bout these mi - ra-cles.
re - det wird hier viel da - von,
Then — noth-ing hap-pens.
doch ge-sche'n tut gar nichts.
Assunta (liberamente)
A'ta
Shame on you! How do you ex-pect your child to be cured if you have no faith?
Schäm dich doch! Denkst du, dass dein Kind ge - heilt wer-den kann, wenn du nicht dranglaubst?
mf
13
Carmela
Allegro ma non troppo
Car.
Look at me! For three years I could - n't walk.
Sieh nur mich! Ich war drei Jahr' lang ge - lähmt.
Assunta
(pointing to an old man in the crowd)
A'ta
He was blind and she made him see a -
Er war blind und dank ihr kann er jetzt
Allegro ma non troppo

Car.
A'ta
There's no doubt she's a saint. Ev.-'ry Ho-ly Fri-day she
Ei-ne Heil-'ge ist sie. Je-den Kar-frei-tag er-
gain.
sehn.
p subito
suf-fers the Pas-sion of Our Lord.
lebt sie die Lei-den Uns-res Herrn.
And that is not all, that is not
Und was sie sonst noch al-les er-
14
Once she saw Saint Mi-chael with two young arch-an-gels.
Mal sah sie Sankt Mi-chael mit zwei jun-gen Erz-en-geln.
all.
lebt.
poco rit.
a tempo
p dolce

Car.
Once she saw the saints and the angels sing and dance all a -
Mal sah sie die Heil - 'gen und En - gel, wie sie san - gen und
round the throne of Our Lord.
tanz - ten un den Thron des Herrn.
15
Assunta
A'ta
Once she saw Saint Pe - ter with the Keys of Heav - en.
Mal sah sie Sankt Pe - ter mit dem gros - sen Schlüs - sel.
Car.
A'ta
Once the Ho - ly Vir - gin ap - peared to her and said she must
Mal ist ihr die Jung - frau er - schie - nen und hat sie zu ih - rem

Car.
A'ta
Once, as she was pray - ing, the
Ein - mal hat der Teu - fel beim
al-ways pray to Her Son.
Sohn zu be - ten er - mahnt.
Dev-il came and set her clothes on fire.
Be-ten ihr das Kleid in Brand ge - steckt.
Al-ways where she goes, one can
Wo sie geht und steht, riecht man
16
She's a dove, she's a burn-ing
Weis - se Tau-be! Lo - dernd heis - se
smell the sweet-est scent of flowers.
im-mer süs - sen Blum-en-duft.
She's a dove, she's a burn-ing

Car.
flame, she's a li - ly, she's the cool - ing
Flam - - me! Zar - te Li - lie! Sanf - te, küh - le
A'ta
flame, she's a li - ly, she's the cool - ing
Car.
wave, she's the cho - sen one, she's the cho -
Wel - - le! Au - ser - wähl - te du, Aus - er - wähl -
A'ta
wave, she's the cho - sen one, she's the cho -
Wel - le! Aus - er - wähl - te du, Aus - er - wähl -
Car.
- sen one
- te du!
Once her broth - er
Ein - mal als ihr
17
A'ta
- sen one
- te du!
Once her broth - er Mi - chel
Ein - mal als ihr Bru - der
poco rit.
pp a tempo

Car.
Mi - chel cursed the Vir - gin Ma ry
Bru - der auf Ma - ri - a fluch - te,

A'ta
cursed the Vir - gin Ma - ry and that ver - y day some - one
auf Ma - ri - a fluch - te, wein - te zur glei - chen Stun - de dies

Car.
and that ver - y day some - one saw that im - age weep tears of
wein - te zur glei - chen Stun - de dies Bild der Jung - frau Trä - nen von

A'ta
saw that im - age there, on the wall, weep tears of
Bild der Jung - frau dort an der Wand Trä - nen von

Maria C.

M.C.
Must my poor child die of hun - ger, then, while we wait here all day?
Lohnt es sich wirk - lich, hier rum - zu - stehn, bis mein Kind vor Hun - ger stirbt?

Car.
blood.
Blut.

A'ta
blood.
Blut.

pp

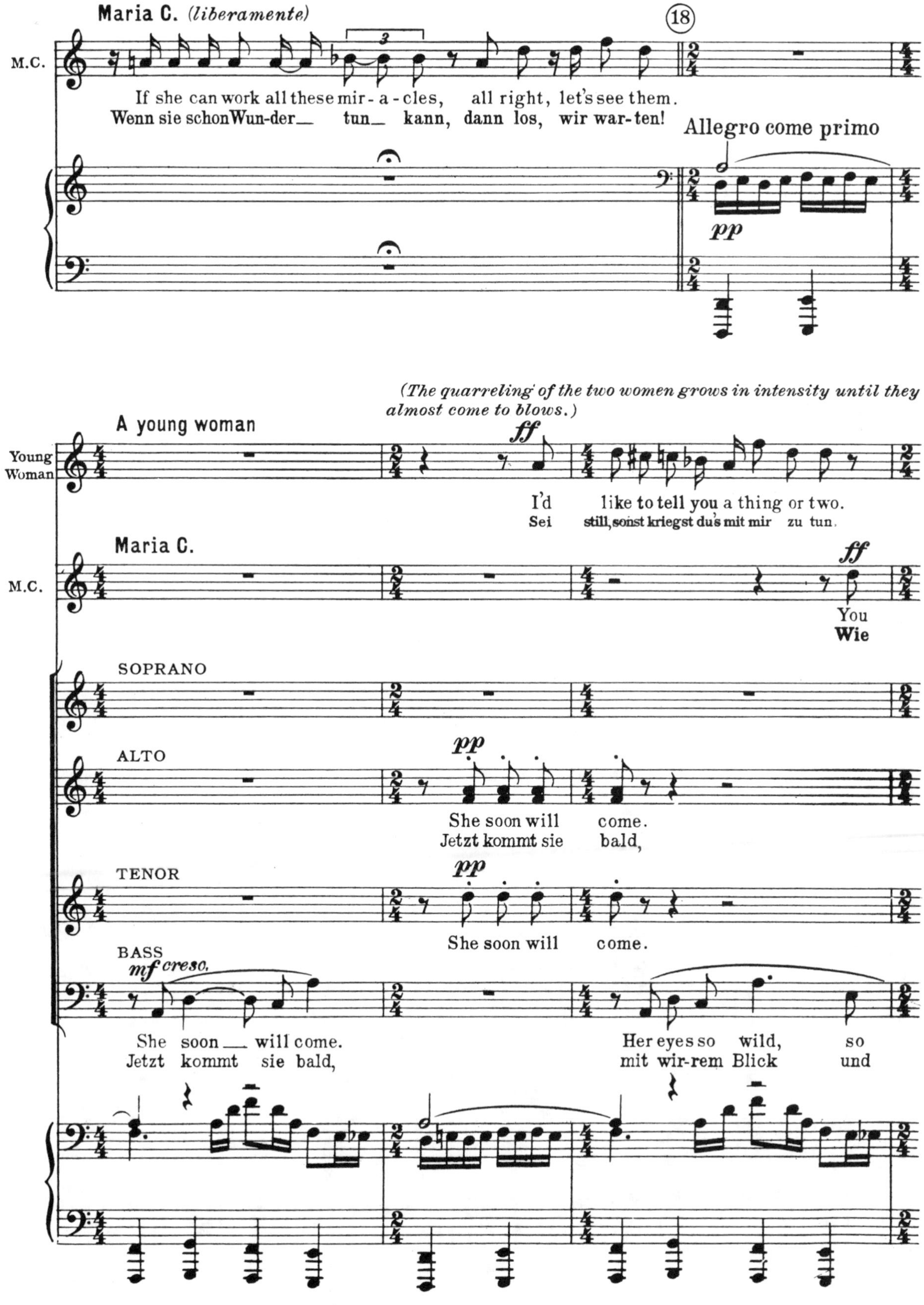

(The quarreling of the two women grows in intensity until they almost come to blows.)

A young woman

Young Woman

ff

I'd like to tell you a thing or two.

Sei still, sonst kriegst du's mit mir zu tun.

Maria C.

M.C.

ff

You

Wie

SOPRANO

ALTO

pp

She soon will come.

Jetzt kommt sie bald,

TENOR

pp

She soon will come.

BASS

mf cresc.

She soon _ will come.

Jetzt kommt sie bald,

Her eyes so wild, so

mit wir-rem Blick und

Young Woman
I'm get - ting sick of
Ich werd noch krank vor
M.C.
shut your mouth and mind your busi - ness.
wär's wenn du die Schnau - ze hiel - test.
Look down, O Lord, up - on Your
Schau nie - der, Va - ter, auf Dein
pale her cheeks.
schmer-zens - bleich.
Young Woman
you! If you are tired, all right, go home. Leave us a - lone. Get out of
aus! Wenn dir's nicht passt, dann geh nach Haus. Lass uns al - lein. Scher dich doch
M.C.
Is
Gib
child. Con-sumed by love, she lies in wait. Oh, blind her eyes with ho - ly
Kind. Es war - tet hier, von Lieb' ver - zehrt. Schenk ihr - em Au - ge heil - ge

19
Young Woman
here! If you don't go, I'll throw you out.
weg! Ver - schwin-de jetzt, sonst setzt es was.
M.C.
this your home by an - y chance? Ah, —
hier nur nicht so schreck-lich an.
Oh, Saint An - ni - na,
Heil - 'ge An - ni - na,
sight and pierce her hands with sa - cred wounds. Saint An - ni - na,
Kraft und Chris - ti Wun - den ih - rer Hand. Heil'ge An - ni - na,
Young Woman
And yap - pi - ty, yap - pi - ty, yap - pi - ty yap!
Ha ha, ha ha ha, ha ha ha ha ha ha.
M.C.
you make me laugh. Ah, —
da lach' ich nur.
daugh - ter of Christ, you bear His Pas - sion,
Toch - ter des Herrn, du trägst Sein Lei - den,

Young Woman
Why don't you let me say my prayer in
Lass mich in Ruh', weil ich jetzt be - ten
M.C.
you make me laugh. You
da lach' ich nur. Ja,
you bear His Light. Come and bless us,
du trägst Sein Licht. Komm und seg - ne uns,
Come,
Komm
Come and bless us,
Come,
Young Woman
peace? And you'll be there to let me in, you
will. Doch du bist dann schon lan-ge drin du
M.C.
pray all day be - cause you're a-fraid of going to Hell.
bet so-viel du willst, in die Höl-le kommst du doch.
ff
come and heal us. Come.
komm und hei - le uns. Komm
f
Come
come and heal us. Come.
f
come

20

Young Woman: strum - pet, you!
Hu - re, du!

M.C.: Be care - ful what you say in front of
Nimm Rück - sicht auf dies un - schulds - vol - le

pp subito
A sud - den chill has filled the
Ganz plötz - lich wird es ei - sig

pp subito

pp subito
A sud - den chill has filled the

pp subito

pp subito

Young Woman: I bet that you don't ev - en know who's the fa - ther of your
Der Ban - kert da. Du weisst ja nicht mal, wer der Va - ter da - von

M.C.: my child. You
Kind hier. Du

room. The light has changed, the clock is still. The sweet-est per - fume fills the
kalt. Das Licht wird blass, die Uhr steht still. Ein süs - ser Duft er - füllt den

room. The light has changed, the clock is still. The sweet-est per - fume fills the

Young Woman
child!
ist.
M.C.
dir - ty bitch! How dare you say such a thing! I bet there is - n't a man on Bleeck-er
Dreck- sau, du! Jetzt wird mir's a - ber zu - viel! Da - bei gibt's si - cher hier kei-nen Mann, mit
air. I'm feel - ing ill, I'm go-ing to faint. There! I hear some voi - ces.
Raum. Ich fühl' mich krank, mir wird so schwach. Da! Ich hö - re Stim - men.
air. I'm feel - ing ill, I'm go-ing to faint. There! I hear some voi - ces.
cresc. poco a poco
Young Woman
Ah! You poi-soned old snake. I'll fix you. If
Al - te Gift-schlan - ge, du! Dir zeig' ich's. Ich
M.C.
Street who has-n't slept with you!
dem du nicht ge-schla-fen hast!
Don't push me!
Die Hand weg!
Yes! Some-one is com - ing. Yes! The door is open-ing.
Ja! Ich glaub, sie kom - men. Ja! Jetzt geht die Tür auf.
Take care! Take care!
Ach - tung! Ach - tung!
Yes! Some-one is com - ing. Yes! The door is open-ing.
Take care! Take care!

Young Woman
you don't leave, I'll wring your neck!
bring dich um, wenn du nicht gehst!

M.C.
Oh ___ let's see you try it!
Oh ___ das möcht ich se-hen!

Oh! I feel I'm going to faint. Come, ___
O Gott, mir wird so schwach. Komm, ___

Oh God! Come, ___
Ach-tung!

Yes! The door is open-ing. Come, ___
Ja! Jetzt geht die Tür auf. Komm, ___

Take care! Come, ___
Ach-tung!

come. ___
komm. ___

come. ___

come. ___
komm. ___

come. ___

21
(Don Marco suddenly appears on the threshold of the bedroom. At his appearance the crowd draws
Don Marco
D.M.
The vi-sion has be - gun.
Die Vi-sion-en fan - gen an.
Lento ma non troppo
back. Some rise in respect—others turn away to hide their eagerness.)
We shall car-ry An-ni-na out.
Gleich brin-gen wir sie her-aus.
But I warn you, you must be-have.
Und ich bitt euch hal-tet euch zu-rück.
She's ver-y ill.
Sie lei-det sehr.
Should she once a-gain be blessed with
Soll - ten sich auch heu - te wie - der die
p dolce

22

D.M.

the stig - ma - ta, be gen - tle with her. Re - mem - ber how great her

Stig-ma-ta zei - gen, nehmt Rück-sicht auf sie, und denkt stets da - ran, was

(*liberamente*)

D.M.

suf - fer - ing must be. If an - y one of you goes near her

sie er - dul - den muss. Wenn ir-gend je-mand ihr zu nah kommt

mf

D.M.

and tries to touch her bleed - ing wounds, I'll throw all of you out of here.

und ih - re Wun-den gar be - rührt, dann werf' ich euch al - le hier raus.

(Don Marco disappears into the bedroom. Shortly

D.M.

Make room for her, and pray.

Macht Platz für sie und be-tet.

pp

p espr.

rall.

after, he re-enters the room followed by two of the neighbors carrying the semi-conscious Annina, whose
23
Adagio ma non troppo
p
mf
p
face is very pale and bears the marks of great suffering.)
f
pp
24
SOPRANO I
(Gently she is placed in a cushioned chair near the center of the stage.
SOPRANO II
p dolcissimo e legato
Sal - ve Vir-go
ALTO
p dolcissimo e legato
Sal - ve Vir-go flo-rens. Ma - ter il - li - ba - ta. Re-
TENOR
BASS
p dolcissimo e legato
Sal - ve Vir-go flo - rens. Ma-ter il - li -
pp

She remains there, with her eyes closed in death-like stillness. Everyone kneels.)
p dolcissimo e legato
Sal - ve Vir - go
flo - rens. Ma - ter il - li - ba - ta.
gi - - - na cle - men - ti -
p dolcissimo e legato
Sal - ve Vir - go flo - rens. Ma - ter il - li -
ba - ta. Re -
25
flo - rens. Ma - ter il - li - ba - ta.
Re - gi - -
ae. Re - gi - na cle - men - ti -
ba - - - ta. Re - gi - -
gi - na cle - men - ti - ae, Re - gi - na cle -

Re - gi - - na cle - men - - ti - ae.
- - na cle - - men - ti - - ae.
ae, cle - - men - ti - - ae.
na cle - men - - ti - ae. Stel - lis
men - ti - ae.
26
p dolciss.
Stel - lis co - ro - na - - - ta. Su - per
p
Stel - lis co - ro - na - - - ta Su - per
p
Stel - lis co - ro - na - ta. Su - per
p
co - ro - na - - - - ta. Su - per
p
Stel - lis co - ro - na - ta Su - per

om-nes an-ge-los pu-ra et im-ma-co-la-ta. At-que ad
om-nes an-ge-los pu-ra et im-ma-co-la-ta. At-que ad
om-nes an-ge-los pu-ra et im-ma-co-la-ta. At-que ad
re-gis dex-te-ram stans ves-te dia-ma-ta per te
re-gis dex-te-ram stans ves-te dia-ma-ta per te
re-gis dex-te-ram stans ves-te dia-ma-ta per te
f
pp

ff
Ma-ter gra-ti-ae dul-cis spes re-o-rum ful-gens stel-la
Ma-ter gra-ti-ae dul-cis spes re-o-rum ful-gens stel-la
Ma-ter gra-ti-ae dul-cis spes re-o-rum ful-gens stel-la
27
(As if pierced by an arrow Annina emits a stifled cry, her body suddenly convulsed by pain.)
ma-ris.
ma-ris.
ma-ris.
ma-ris.
fff

28
Lento
Annina
(Still with eyes closed and a tormented expression on her face, as if fighting a fearful force.)
Ann.
Oh, Sweet Je - sus, spare me this a - go - ny.
Oh, mein Je - sus, er las - se mir die - se Qual.
p
Too great a pain is this for one so weak
Ich bin nicht stark ge - nug für so - viel Leid.
Ah, my ach - ing heart, must you a - gain with - stand the
Muss mein wun - des Herz die Prü - fung noch ein - mal be -
(liberamente)
(opening her eyes)
trial? Where am I? Who are these peo - ple?
stehn? Wo bin ich? Was sind das für Leu - te?

(liberamente)
Ann.
When have I seen this road be-fore,
Wann hab ich die-sen Weg ge-sehn?
ppp
when this bar-ren hill? What is this drunk-en crowd wait-ing for?
Wann den kah-len Berg? Wor-auf war-tet die trun-ke-ne Men-
29
ge?
Ah, dread-ful pre-sen-ti-ment!
Ah, schreck-li-che Ah-nun-gen!
f
ff
p
Lento e pesante
(She gets up as if in a trance and slowly moves through the kneeling neighbors.)
Ea-ger and loud, they push and sway under the fes-ti-val sun.
Gie-rig und joh-lend drängt das Volk, grad als wär heu-te ein Fest.
Tpt.
p lontano
pp

Ann.
What do they want?
Wo woll'n sie hin?
What are they wait - ing for?
Und wor - auf war - ten sie?
poco a poco accel. fine al Moderato e sostenuto
(She moves her arms as if fighting her way through a crowd.)
Ann.
I can - not see.
Ich se - he nichts.
Eh! Don't push me.
He! Macht Platz da.
Tpt.
più vicina
cresc. poco a poco
Ann.
Let me see. Please make room for me.
Lasst mich sehn. Bit-te, Lasst mich da - hin.
Oh! Oh!

Moderato e sostenuto
30
Ann.
I see now,—
Jetzt seh ich,
I see now!
jetzt seh ich!
f
8
Oh, blinding sight!
Oh, Schrek-kens-bild!
Oh, pain! Oh, love!
Oh Schmerz! Oh Lie-be!
ff
6
3
fff

31
Con moto
(staring intently ahead)
Ann.
They come up the bend-ing road in
Dort um die Ec-ke kom-men sie, in
p dolente
gold-en ar-mor, the sol-diers, and a-mong them a pur-ple cloak. My
gold-ner Rüs-tung, Sol-da-ten, und da-zwi-schen ein ro-tes Ge-wand. Mein
Je-sus! How large a cross for one man to bear! Dust in His mouth and salt of bit-ter
Je-sus! Wie schwer die Last des Kreu-zes Ihn drückt! Staub auf dem Mund und Salz von bit-tren
rit.
a tempo
tears. His cheeks rib-boned with blood shed by the sharp and cru-el crown.
Trä-nen. Die Wan-gen vol-ler Blut, das von der Dor-nen-krone fli-esst.

Ann.
Ah!
But His eyes!
Sei - ne Au -
p dolce
32
Who ev-er saw in a man's eyes such pa-tient love?
gen! Wer sah in ei-nes Men-schen Aug' je so-viel Lie - be?
Ah! He fal-ters. They are on Him with whips. He strug-gles on a-gain.
Er strau-chelt. Sie schla-gen auf Ihn ein. Er rafft sich wie-der auf.
f
33
(Suddenly disturbed, her eyes search through the imaginary crowd.)
Some-one is weep-ing. Where? I
Ich hö-re Wei-nen. Wo nur? Jetzt
pp

poco più mosso
Ann.
see now— a group of wail - ing wo - men stand-ing be-hind the crowd.
seh ich's,— ein Häuf-lein wei-nen der Frau-en hin - ter dem viel - en Volk.
mf espr.
Weak-ened by weep-ing, they sway like reeds as they slow-ly
El - end vom Wei - nen, schwan-ken sie vor Schmerz wie das Rohr im
34
move. Tall a-mongst them, Her eyes deep-ened by pain, the Ho-ly Vir-gin stands.
Wind. In ih - re Mit-te den Blick dun-kel vor Schmerz, seh ich Ma-ri - a stehn.
Why, Ma-ry, why did you come? No cross can weigh nor nail can pierce as
Wa - rum, Ma - ri - a kamst du her? Das Kreuz ist zu schwer, der Na-gel zu spitz für
p

Ann.
35
can a moth-er's sor - row. Why, Ma - ry, why did you come?
f
poco rit.
a tempo
O wo-men, take her home
36
When our God will die, on-ly her Son will bear the a - go-ny. Oh,
f

Ann.
take her, — take her home. It is her ver-y flesh that will be torn by spear and
bringt sie, bringt sie heim. Es wird ihr ei-gen Fleisch mit spit-zen Nä-geln hier durch-
nail. Oh, take her, take her home.
bohrt. Oh, bringt sie, bringt sie heim.
ff
Oh wo-men, take her home. No hill was ev - er high-er.
Ihr Frau-en bringt sie heim. Kein Berg war je so hoch,
37
rall.
p
mf

38
Ann.
The whole world can
die gan - ze Welt kann
f
8

Ann.
see the Son of God, sweet Je - sus,
Got-tes Sohn hier sehn, Ihn, Je - sus,
8

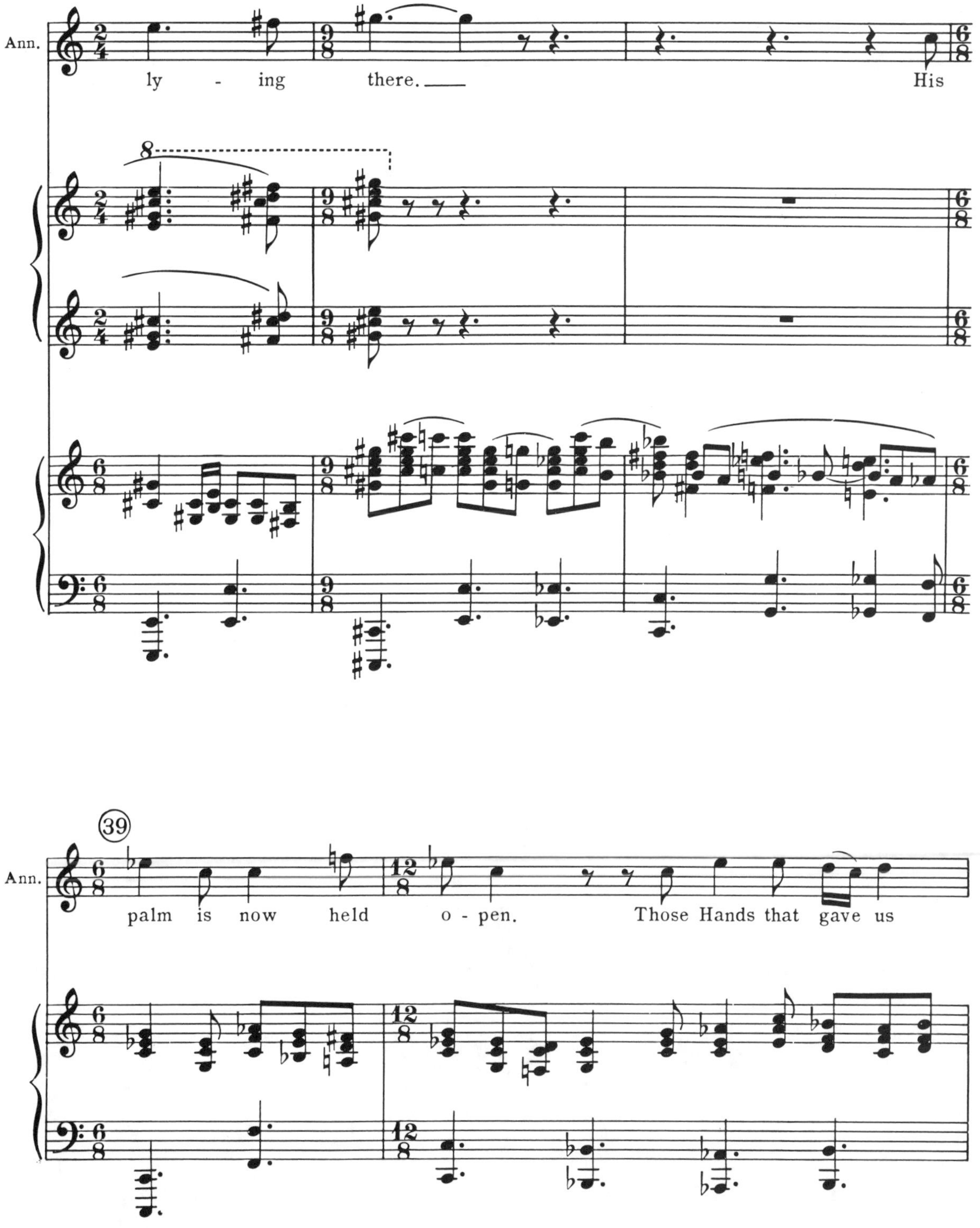
Ann.
ly - ing there. His
8
39
Ann.
palm is now held o - pen. Those Hands that gave us

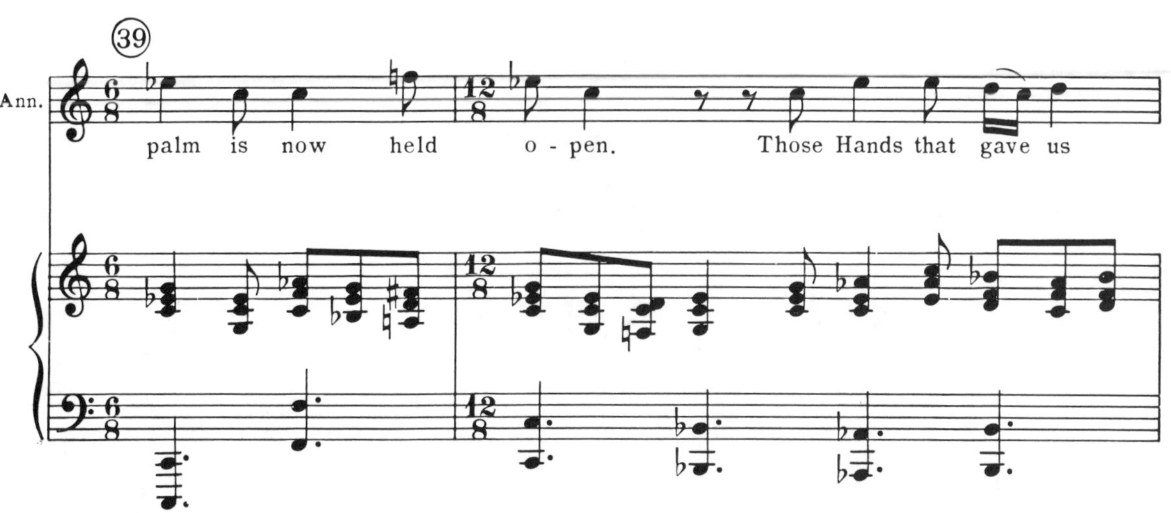

Ann.
all, by us are to be pierced.
heil - ten, von uns wer - den sie durchbohrt.
Ann.
Sol - dier, sol - dier, have mer - cy on
Ach, Sol - da - ten, habt Mit - lied mit
p
mf
6
3
Ann.
40
Him. For He a - lone is your
Ihm, denn er ist eu - er Er -
8
loco
f
4
3

Ann.
Sa - viour.
lö - ser.
The nail is held in place.
Man setzt den Na-gel an.
ff
ff
(With a piercing cry she falls back on the pillows.)
41
Ann.
The huge ham-mer is raised. Ah
Und jetzt hebt man den Ham-mer.
ff
pesantissimo ma poco più mosso
fff

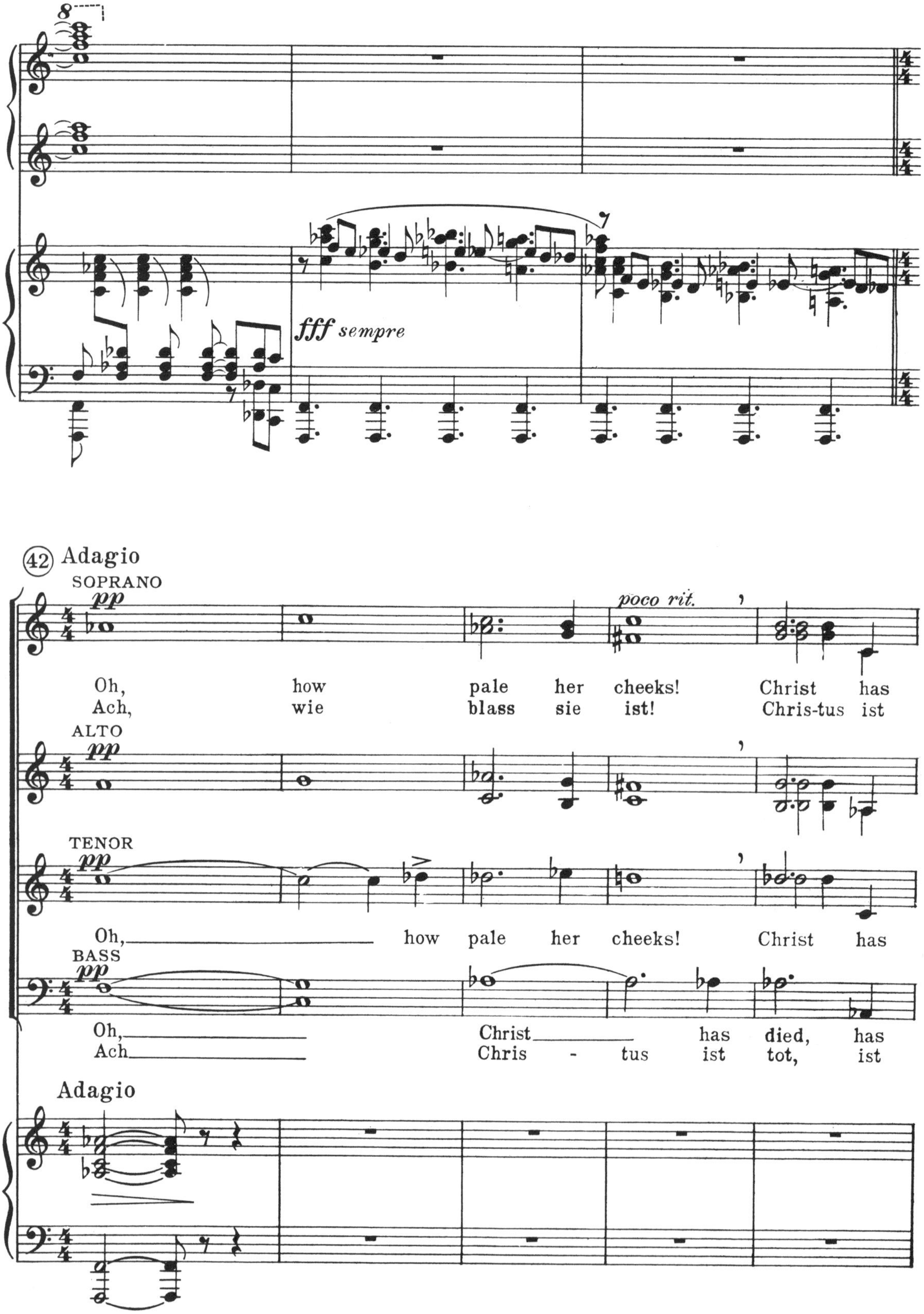

(42) Adagio

SOPRANO

pp

poco rit.

Oh, how pale her cheeks! Christ has

Ach, wie blass sie ist! Chris-tus ist

ALTO

pp

TENOR

pp

Oh, how pale her cheeks! Christ has

BASS

pp

Oh, Christ has died, has

Ach Chris - tus ist tot, ist

Adagio

(Annina's limp hands slowly open, revealing the bleeding stigmata.)

Allegro

died. — Look! The stig-ma - ta! The
tot. — Seht! Die Stig-ma - ta! Das

The

died. — Look! The stig-ma - ta!
Seht! Die Stig-ma-ta!

Allegro

pp *p* *cresc.*

(thud)

mir - a - cle has hap pened, mir a cle has hap-pened. The ho - ly wounds are
Wun-der ist ge-sche-hen, ja, es ist ge - sche - hen. Die heil - gen Wun - den

mir - a - cle has hap-pened. The ho - ly wounds are
Wun - der ist ge - sche - hen.

The mir - a - cle has hap-pened, it
Das Wun-der ist ge - sche - hen, es

The mir - a - cle has
Das Wun - der ist ge -

f

bleed-ing, The ho - ly wounds are bleed-ing.
blu - ten, die heil - 'gen Wun - den blu - ten.
bleed-ing. She nev - er lets us down.
blu - ten, Sie lässt uns nie im Stich.
has hap-pened.
ist ge-sche - hen.
Let me touch her,
Lasst mich sie be-rüh - ren,
hap-pened. The ho - ly wounds are bleed - ing. Let me touch her,
sche-hen. Die heil-'gen Wun - den blu - ten.
43
Let me touch her, let me, let me. Oh!
Lasst mich sie be-rüh-ren, lasst mich, lasst mich.
let me, let me. Oh!
ff

(The neighbors crowd around Annina trying hysterically to touch her while Don Marco, Assunta, and Carmela vainly fight to keep back the crowd.)

44
has no mon - ey and my child - ren have no cloth - ing.
kei - ne Ar - beit, uns - re Kin - der geh'n in Lum - pen.
with a fam - i - ly of sev - en and my wife is ver - y, ver - y
sie - ben - köp - fi - ger Fa - mi - lie, und da - zu 'ne sehr schwer kran - ke
Oh!
Oh!
ill! Oh!
Frau.

(Maria Corona pushes her dumb son through the struggling crowd. He approaches Annina and touches her bleeding hand.)

45
Oh,
Oh,
Oh.
Oh,
Oh,
Oh.
It is my turn now,
Lasst mich nach vor - ne,
it is my turn now.
Lasst mich nach vor - ne.
Bless me!
Seg-ne mich!
Bless me!
Seg-ne mich!
Oh!
Bless me! It is my turn.
Ich bin jetzt dran.
Bless me! It is my turn.
Ich bin jetzt dran.

46
(Michele has suddenly appeared at the door which leads to the street.)
Michele
(gridato)
Mich.
Stop it!
Schluss da-mit!
Bless me! Bless me!
Seg-ne mich! Seg-ne mich!
Bless me! Bless me!
Seg-ne mich! Seg-ne mich!
sfff
pesante
ff
(liberamente)
Out of here, all of you! What do you think this is... a mar-ket place?
Raus mit euch, raus mit euch! Was glaubt ihr, was hier ist? Ein Wo-chen-markt?
ff
Carmela
(Intimidated, the crowd falls back)
Car.
She's ver-y ill. Be gen-tle with her.
Sie ist sehr krank. Sei freund-lich zu ihr.
Michele
(to Carmela)
lunga
Leave my sis - ter a-lone! How is she?
Lasst meine Schwes-ter in Ruh! Wie geht's ihr?

47
(Michele approaches Annina and tenderly caresses her hair.)
Andante con moto
Michele
(liberamente)
(to the crowd)
Mich.
Clowns! Leech-es!
Töl-pel! Klet - ten!
pp
ff
Fa-nat-ics! Out of here,quick! Shall I call the po-lice?
Ihr Frömm-ler! Raus mit euch,marsch! Ich hol die Po - li - zei.
Out, out!
Raus, raus!
48
(With the help of Carmela, Michele carries Annina back into her room, while the neighbors slowly leave. Only Don Marco remains.)
Allegro ma non troppo
For- give him, O Lord!
Ver - gib ihm, o Herr!
He drowns our sun.
Er löscht un-sre Son - ne.
He bars the light from
Er sperrt uns ab vom
Allegro ma non troppo
pp
p
8

Have mer-cy on him!
Er - bar-me dich sein!
pp
Oh!
Heav-en's gates.
Him-mels-licht.
8
49
He fears our Faith.
Er hast uns-ern Glau -
For-
Ver-
Oh!

He fears to meet the eyes of God.
Er scheut sich, Gott in's Aug' zu sehn.
give him, O Lord!
gib ihm, o Herr!
Have mer-cy on
Er - bar-me dich
8
Oh!
Oh!
him,
sein,
Have mer-cy on him.
er - bar-me dich sein!

Have mer - cy on him!
Er - bar - me dich sein!
Have mer - cy on him!
8
pp
50
(Michele re-enters the room and hostilely faces Don Marco.)
Andante, molto sostenuto
poco rit.
ff
mf
Michele (liberamente)
Mich.
And you, priest, why don't you go? How oft - en must I tell you
Und Sie, Herr Pfar-rer, was woll'n Sie noch? Sie soll - ten lang - sam wis - sen,
p

Mich.
that you're not want - ed here?
Sie sind hier un - er-wünscht.
Don Marco
D.M.
I on - ly came when I was called. Your
Ich kom-me nur, wenn man mich ruft. Ih-re
Doc-tors she needs, rath-er than priests and can- dles.
Ärz-te braucht sie, doch kei-nen Pries - ter und Ker- zen.
sis - ter need-ed me.
Schwes-ter brauch-te mich.
51
(liberamente)
If we were rich this would-n't hap-pen. Rich
Es liegt nur da - ran, dass wir nicht reich sind, sonst

Mich.
people have no vi-sions ex-cept in hos-pi-tals.
hätt' sie ihre Vi-si-o-nen in ei-nem Kran-ken-haus.
D.M.
And you, who love her so,
Grad Sie, der Sie sie lie-
Andante
p
— you are the one to doubt.
ben soll-ten an ihr nicht zwei-feln.
Too much I love her not to know her
Grad weil ich sie lie-be, kenn ich sie so ge-
well. A sick-ly child who nev-er grew. A sim-ple
nau. Als Kind schon war sie zart und schwach, ei-ne schlich-te
8

Mich.
D.M.
mind— in a pain-pierced bod-y.
See - le in ei-nem kran-ken Kör-per.
(a tempo)
Who knows where God will find His
Wer weiss, wo Gott ei-ne Heil'-ge
poco rall.
52
Allegro ma non troppo
accel.
His saints? E-nough of su-per - sti-tion! Who
Heil' - ge? Für a-ber-glaüb'-ge Wei-ber! Wer
saints?
sucht?
Allegro ma non troppo
mf secco
are— these peo-ple who cre-ate— your saints? They
ist es denn, der eu - re Heil' - gen macht? Nur

Mich.
wor - ship God out of de - feat. They
Leu - te, die fromm sind weil sie in Not sind. Nur
look for won-ders to for - get their pov - er - ty,
Leu - te, die auf Wun-der war - ten weil sie die Ar - mut drückt.
53
to re - deem their fai-lure. But I am not re-signed,
Nur ge-schei-ter-te Ex-i - sten-zen. Doch ich ge-hör' nicht da-zu,
ff
mp
(Suddenly confronts Don Marco.)
Andante
liberamente
nor am I con-quered yet. Tell me, o priest, do
ich bin noch nicht be - siegt. Ganz un-ter uns, glau-ben
ff
mf
f
l.h.

(liberamente)
Mich.
you be-lieve in this? Is this the work of God, — or the de-lu-sions of a sick mind?
Sie an dies al-les? Sind das hier Wer-ke Got-tes o-der Symp-to-me ei-ner Krank-heit?
p
Don Marco
D.M.
54
Allegro ma non troppo
A priest is not a judge but on-ly a guide. I do not say that
Ein Prie-ster ist kein Rich-ter er ist nur ein Hirt. Es ist ganz gleich, ob
D.M.
I be-lieve in this, but she be-lieves and must be guid-ed.
ich dran glau-be. Sie a-ber glaubt, und ich muss sie be-hü-ten.
Michele
Mich.
If one must guide her, then I shall be her guide, for
Wenn sie be-schützt wer-den muss, dann tu-e ich's, denn

Mich.
I am her broth - er.
ich bin ihr Bru - der.
55
I warn you, priest,
Ich war-ne Sie,
D.M.
So are we all.
Das sind wir al - le.
f
pp
ff
Mich.
keep a - way from us.
Sie be - läst' gen uns.
For I a -
Denn ich nur
ff
Mich.
lone shall guide my sis - ter,
lei - te mei - ne Schwes-ter,
and I shall save her yet from
und ich be-schüt-ze sie vor
your fan - a - tic hun-ger.
eu - rem Fan - a - tis-mus.
Mol-
ff
ff

to marcato
56
Adagio ma non troppo
D.M.
Ah, poor Mi-che-le, it is not I your ri-val, but
Ar-mer Mi-che-le, nicht ich bin Ihr Ri-va-le, son-dern
D.M.
God Him-self, And what hu-man love can com-pete with the love for God?
Gott selbst. Und was gilt die Lie-be zu Men-schen ge-gen die Lie-be zu Gott?
D.M.
How can one fight what can-not be mea-sured? Who can hold back the
Wie kann man ge-gen Un-mess-ba-res kämp-fen? Wer hält den Blitz, den

D.M.
a - va - lanche or quench the rag-ing fire?
Don-ner-schlag o-der die La-wi-ne auf?
What God de - crees
Was Gott be-stimmt,
D.M.
we can on - ly wit-ness.
dess' sind wir nur Zeu - ge.
57
Who, by God's love is
Wen Got-tes Lie-be ver-
rit.
a tempo
espr.
pp
D.M.
wound - ed and by its tide en - cir - cled, is then for - ev - er
wun - det, wen Got - tes Lie - be ge - zeich - net, der bleibt für al - le

D. M.
poco rall.
58
(Don Marco leaves and Michele slams the door after him.)
drawn into its tu-mul-tu-ous vor - tex.
Zeit in Sei-nen u-nent-rinn-ba-ren Krei - sen.
a tempo
poco riten.
ff
poco rall.
a tempo
a tempo
poco riten.
poco riten.
a tempo
mf espr.
Curtain
p

(59) Allegro

cresc.

(60)

f

61
ff
8

62
8
tr
Molto tenuto
63
fff
8
8
64

65
66
mf dolce
r. h.
f
mf dolce
r. h.
p

Scene II

(An empty lot on Mulberry Street, flanked by tenement houses. The lot is enclosed by an old, wire fence with a gate leading to the street, which is festively decorated with arches of electric bulbs. All through this scene passersby and street vendors will be seen in the background. Inside the lot, Annina and Carmela are sitting on empty crates near the steps leading to the back door of the tenement house, stage left. Armed with scissors, needles and gold paper-maché, they are sewing stars on the white gown of Concettina, a pathetic, little girl about 5 years old, primitively dressed as an angel. Assunta is seen at one of the windows, rocking her baby to sleep. It is late afternoon.)

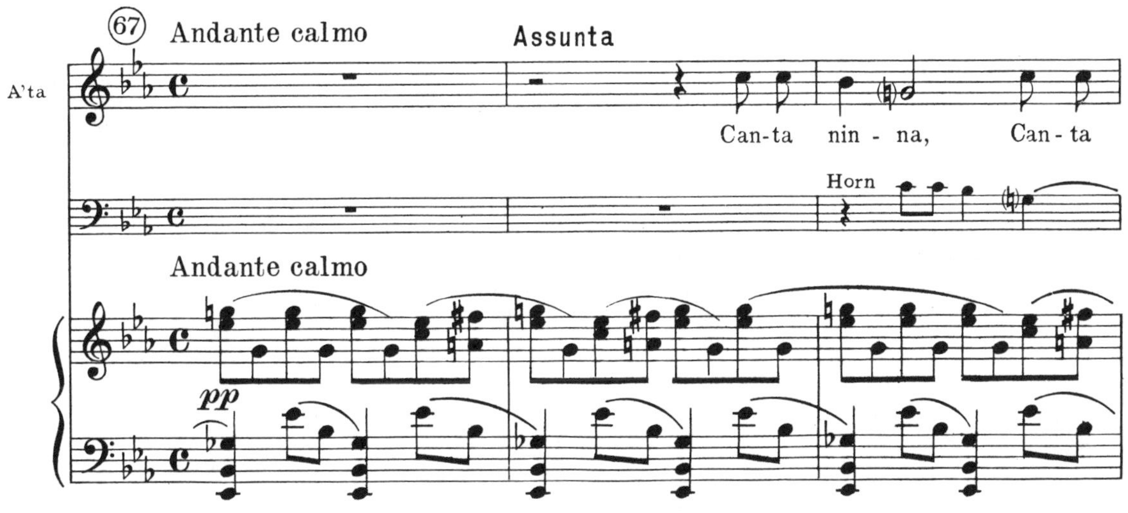

(A group of women, dressed in loud flowery prints enters, from the back door of the other tenement house, stage right.)
One Woman
(screaming up to a window)
Woman
Re - na - ta,
A'ta
pos - sa ad - dor - men - tar. Mam - ma de - ve, mam - ma
Woman
Re - na - ta!
E
Girl (at the window)
Girl
What's the mat - ter with you?
Wa - rum schreist du denn so?
A'ta
de - ve scal - dar la ce - na, per - ché Bab - bo, per - ché

Woman
spic-cia-ti dun-que!
6
Good eve'-ing, An-ni-na.
Gu-ten A-bend, An-ni-na.
Girl
Go a-head, I'm com-ing.
Ja, schon gut, ich kom-me.
Annina
Ann.
Good
Gu-ten
A'ta
Bab - bo rin-ca-se - rà. Già si le - van, già si
Woman
7
Aren't you go-ing to the pro-ces-sion?
Gehst du nicht mit zur Pro-zes - sion?
Ann.
eve'-ing.
A - bend.
A'ta
le - van le stel - le in ciel, Già co -

Woman
Ann.
A'ta
(to her friends)
Is-n't it a shame? He's a
Ist das nicht ge-mein? So ein
Oh, no, I can't. My broth-er won't let me.
Nein, heu-te nicht. Mein Bru-der er-laubt's nicht.
min - cia, già co-min-cia ad an-not-tar.
68
(They go out into the street and disappear around the corner.)
Woman
Car.
Ann.
A'ta
brute!
Kerl!
Stand still, Con-cet - ti - na.
Halt still, Con-cet - ti - na.
Stand
Halt
Can - ta nin - na, can - ta

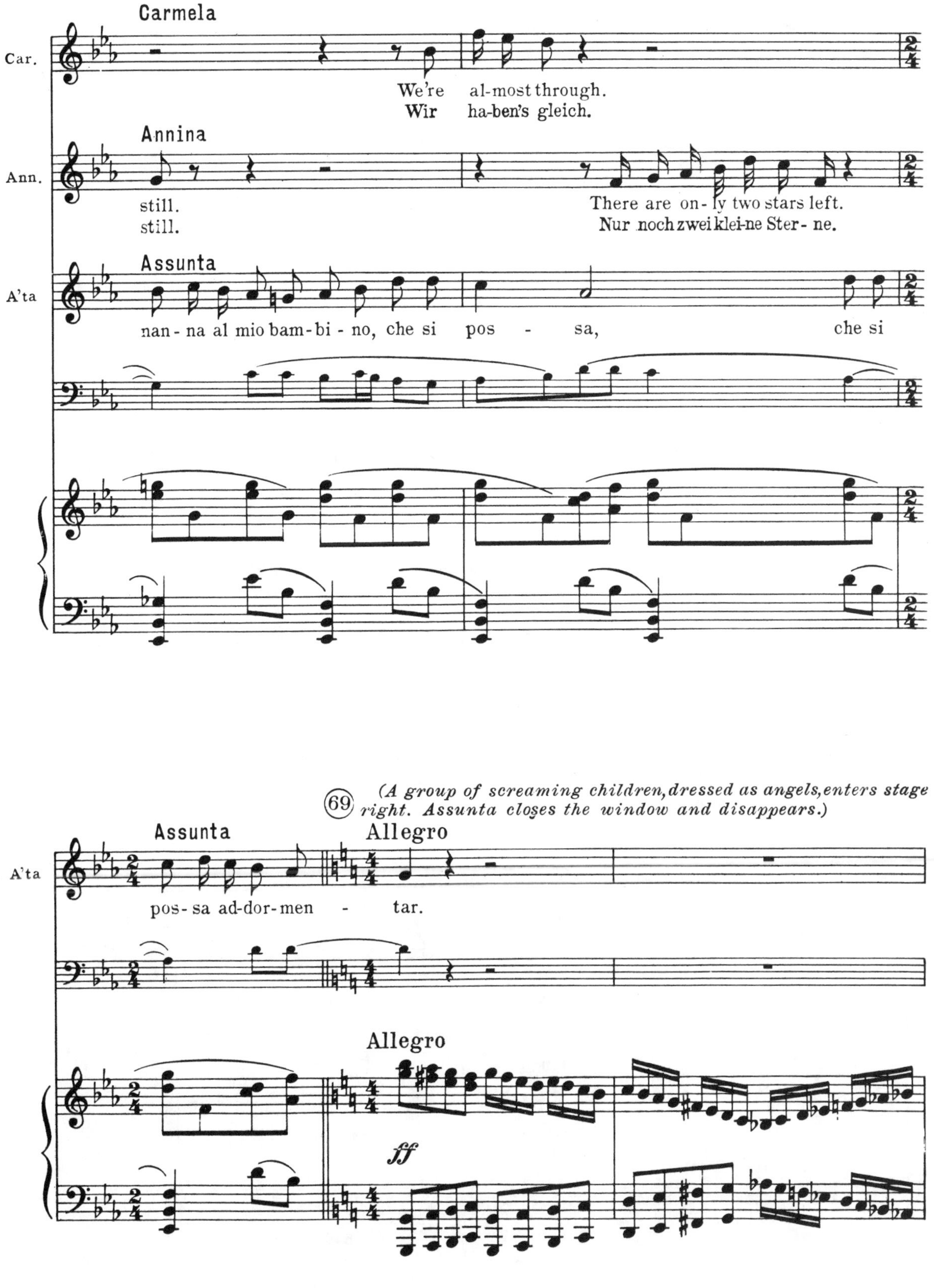

Carmela

Car.

We're al-most through.
Wir ha-ben's gleich.

Annina

Ann.

still. There are on- ly two stars left.
still. Nur noch zwei klei-ne Ster- ne.

Assunta

A'ta

nan- na al mio bam-bi - no, che si pos - sa, che si

„Komm, Concettina, sonst kommst du zu spät!
Children: "Come on, Concettina. You're going to be late!

Los, Concettina, mach schnell!"
Come on, Concettina, hurry up!"
(They run in great confusion toward the

street and disappear, while Concettina jumps up and down with impatience.)

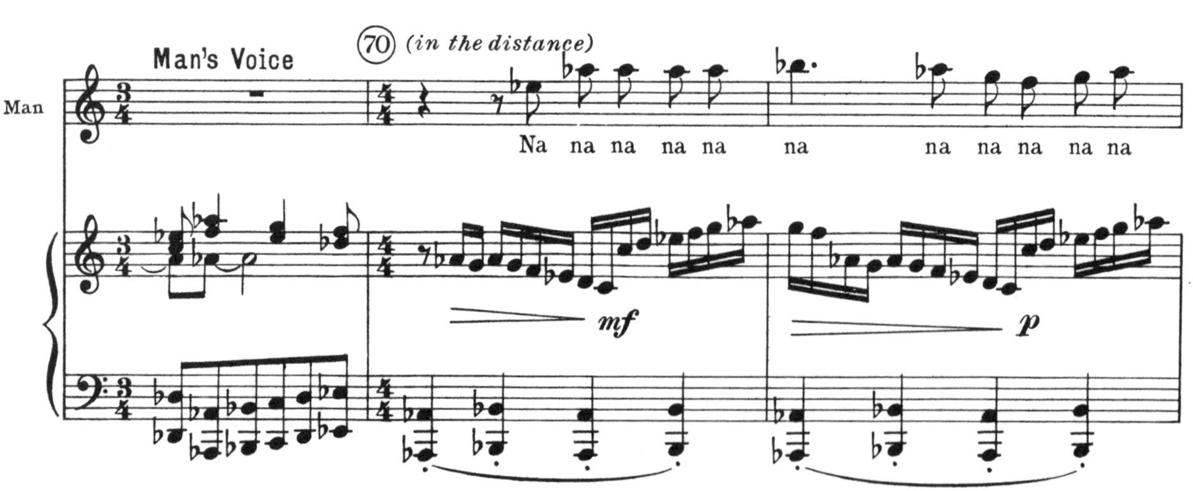
Man's Voice
70
(in the distance)
Man
Na na na na na na na na na na na
mf
p

Man's Voice
71
Un poco meno
Man
na
Woman's Voice
(from far away)
Woman
Con-cet - ti - na!
Carmela
Car.
Be
Mo-
Un poco meno
5
pp
Concettina
(Whining, she tries to pull away from the sewing girls, who hold her back.)
Con.
Eh, let me go . . .
Ich will jetzt weg...
Woman
Con-cet - ti - na!
Car.
pa - tient.
ment noch.
Stand still.
Halt still.
We on - ly have one
Nur ei - nen klei - nen

Annina
Ann.
Then we shall fit the pa-per crown
Dann setz ich dir die Kro-ne auf,
and you will be the pret-tiest
und dann wirst du die Al - ler -
Carmela
Car.
star left.
Stern noch.
mf
Concettina
Con.
Let me go. . .
Ich will weg. . .
Eh! Let me go. . .
Ich will jetzt weg. . .
Woman's Voice
Woman
Con-cet-ti - na!
Annina
Ann.
of them all.
schöns-te sein.
All
Jetzt
Carmela
Car.
p

(Finally freed, but still whining. Concettina runs off toward the street, her angel wings rather limp, and her gold crown askew.)
Annina
Ann.
right, you can go now.
sind wir auch fer - tig.
pp
Carmela
72
Poco meno mosso
Car.
An - ni - na, I've some - thing to con -
An - ni - na, ich muss dir et - was
p
Annina (liberamente)
Why, Car - me - la, what can it be?
Ja, Car - me - la, was hast du denn?
Carmela
fess to you, and I feel so a - shamed.
ein - ge - stehn, und ich schä - me mich so.

Carmela
Car.
Do you re-mem-ber when I prom-ised that one day I'd take the
Ich ha-be dir doch mal ver-spro-chen, dass ich mit dir den
p
Annina
(liberamente)
9
Ann.
Yes, And are-n't you going to take the veil with me?
Ja, das hast du doch auch im-mer vor-ge-habt.
Carmela
Car.
veil with you?
Schlei-er neh-me.
Oh,
Ach,
p
73
Ann.
But why? What has hap-pened?
Wirk-lich? Und wa-rum nicht?
5
Car.
An-ni-na, I'm a-fraid I'm going to break my prom-ise.
An-ni-na, ich fürch-te, ich kann mein Wort nicht hal-ten.
mf

Carmela (shyly)
Car.
This com-ing May I'm going to be mar-ried. Oh, if you knew what it is to be in love.
Im näch-sten Früh-jahr ist un-sre Hoch-zeit. Du weisst ja nicht, was ver-liebt - sein heisst.
p
poco rall.
First I fought it, then I prayed Ho - ly Ma - ry to make me for - get him.
An-fangs sträubt' ich mich, dann hab ich viel ge - be - tet, um ihn zu ver - ges - sen.
poco rall.
a tempo
I thought of him e - ven as I was pray - ing. It was aw - ful, could - n't help it.
So - gar beim Be - ten musst' ich an ihn den - ken. Es war schreck-lich, al - les half nichts.
pp
(liberamente)
His name is Sal - va - to - re. He's such a nice boy.
Er heisst Sal - va - to - re. Er ist wirk - lich lieb.

Car.
(bursting into tears)
Last week he asked me to mar - ry him and I'm a - fraid I said
Ges - tern hat er um mich an-ge-hal-ten. Ich muss ge - stehn, ich sag - te
74
Annina
Ann.
Oh, I am so glad for you! Such hap - py news.
Oh, ich freu mich so für dich! Was für ein Glück!
Car.
yes.
Ja.
f dolce
Ann.
Sil - ly girl, what are you cry-ing for?
Dum-mes Kind du brauchst doch nicht zu wei-nen,
Poco meno mosso
But
Wa-
Car.
But won't God be an - gry with me?
Ach, wird Gott nicht bös auf mich sein?
Poco meno mosso
p

(liberamente)
Ann.
why should He?
rum denn nur?
8
But your prom-ise was-n't made to
Du gabst dein Ver-spre-chen doch nicht
Car.
Be-cause I broke my prom-ise.
Ich hab doch mein Wort ge-bro-chen.
accel.
a tempo
God, on-ly to me. And I re-lease you!
Gott, son-dern nur mir. Und ich lass dich frei!
Oh, sweet An-ni-na!
Lieb-ste An-ni-na!
a tempo
f
75
poco rall.
Yes, if you prom-ise that you will come to mine.
Wenn du ver-sprichst dass du zu mei-ner kommst.
Will you come to my wed-ding?
Kommst du zu mei-ner Hoch-zeit?
poco rall.

Ann.
One day I, too, shall wear a white veil. God is wait - ing for His bride.
Bald trag auch ich den weis - sen Schlei - er. Gott er - war - tet Sei - ne Braut.
Car.
a tempo
poco rall.
Ann.
Car.
Then you think that I still have a chance to go to heav - en?
Al - so glaubst du, ich komm viel - leicht doch noch in den Him - mel?
Assunta (Appears in the doorway and, on hearing Carmela's remarks, bursts out laughing.)
Allegro
(liberamente)
A'ta
Ah! Ah! Ah! Sil - ly goose! When you'll have six chil -
Ha! Ha! Ha! Dum - me Gans! Wenn du sechs Kin - der

A'ta
dren and a drunk-en hus-band like I do, you'll be sure to
hast und ei-nen Säu-fer zum Mann, so wie ich, kommst du auf je-den
go to heav-en when you die!
Fall in den Him-mel, wenn du stirbst!
76
(Rubbing her back and moaning slightly with pain, she sits on the steps next to the two girls.)
f
p
(spoken)
Oh, my back!
Oh, mein Rücken!
Some-times I
Ich möcht wohl
won-der what heav-en must be like.
wis-sen, wie es im Him-mel ist.
Shall I have a chance to
Komm ich dort viel-leicht mal zum
pp

Annina
Ann.
Oh, poor As-sun-ta!
Ar-me As-sun-ta!
Assunta
A'ta
(liberamente)
sleep there?
schla-fen?
Tell me, An-ni-na, did you ev-er get a glimpse of heav-en?
Sag mal, An-ni-na, hast du mal ein Stück vom Him-mel ge-se-hen?

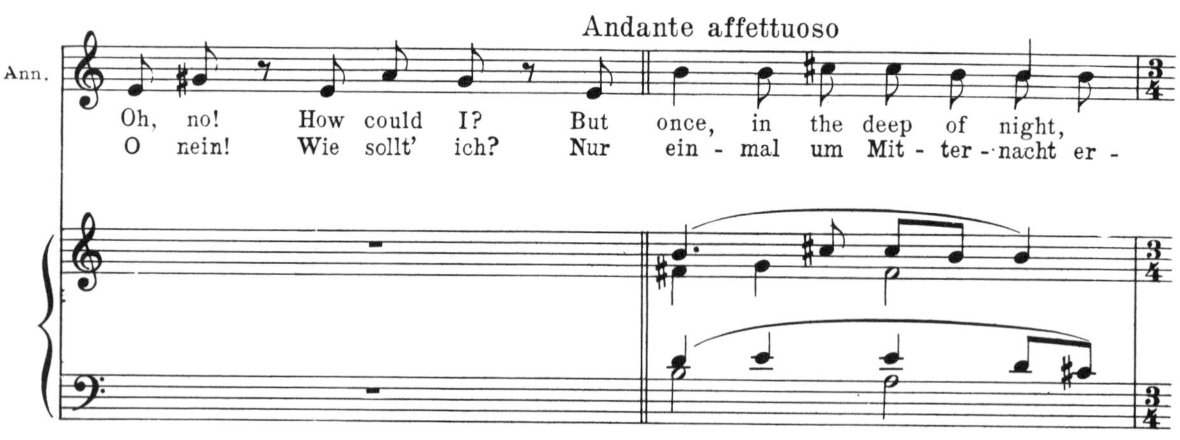
Andante affettuoso
Ann.
Oh, no! How could I? But once, in the deep of night,
O nein! Wie sollt' ich? Nur ein-mal um Mit-ter-nacht er-

77
Ann.
Mi-chael, the Arch-an-gel, came to me. With a smile he said:
schien mir der Erz-en-gel Mi-cha-el. Lä-chelnd sag-te er:

poco rit.
a tempo
Ann.
"What is it you wish, my child?" "An - gel fair, if on - ly I could see the
„Hast du ei-nen Wunsch, mein Kind?" „Ja" sprach ich, „darf ich ein einz-ges Mal das

poco rit.
78
a tempo
Ann.
gold - en gates of Par - a - dise." Oh, how swift was his flight,
gold - ne Tor zum Him - mel sehn?" Oh, wie leicht war sein Flug!

rall.
Ann.
Oh, how soft were his wings. When I woke the blind - ing
Oh, wie sanft sei - ne Hand! Plötz - lich stand ich vor dem
rall.

Annina
a tempo
Ann.
gates stood there.
Him - mels - tor.
Carmela
Car.
Oh, how swift was his flight, Oh, how soft were his wings.
Oh, wie leicht war sein Flug! Oh, wie sanft sei - ne Hand!
Assunta
A'ta
Oh, how swift was his flight, Oh, how soft were his wings.
a tempo
Car.
When she woke the gates of Par-a-dise stood in front of her.
Plötz - lich stand sie vor dem gros - sen, gold - nen Him-mels - tor.
A'ta
When she woke the gates of Par-a-dise stood in front of her.

79
Annina
Ann.
Stand - ing by the gates, sweet, old Saint Pe - ter wel-comed me.
Vor dem To - re stand Pe - trus und nick-te mir freund-lich zu.
"When I die, if I'm re-ceived, what shall I find be-hind your gold-en
„Was," frag-te ich, „er - war - tet mich nach mei-nen Tod dort hin - ter die-sem
poco rit.
80
a tempo
gates?"
Tor?"
"You will eat gold-en bread and wear sun - wo - ven clothes.
„Gold-nes Brot isst du dort, und trägst Klei-der aus Licht.
rit.
a tempo

Annina
Ann.
You will sing the praise of Christ, Our Lord."
Prei-sen wirst du Gott in E - wig - keit."
Carmela
Car.
We shall eat gold - en bread
Gold - nes Brot ess ich dort,
Assunta
A'ta
We shall eat gold - en bread
Ann.
Car.
And wear sun - wo - ven clothes. We shall sing the praise of
und trag Klei - der aus Licht. Prei - sen werd ich Gott, den
A'ta
And wear sun - wo - ven clothes. We shall sing the praise of

(Maria Corona runs in from the street, dragging her dumb son after her.)

Maria Corona

M.C.: An - ni - na, An - ni - na!

Car.: Christ, Our Lord in e - ter - ni - ty.
Herrn in al - le E - wig - keit.

A'ta: Christ, Our Lord in e - ter - ni - ty.

ff agitato

mf

M.C.: I ran all the way. I thought I'd bet - ter warn you. The Vir - gin Ma - ry pro - tect us all!
Ich kann fast nicht mehr. Ich muss - te euch doch war - nen. Die Heil' - ge Jung - frau be - schüt - ze uns!

82

M.C.

There is going to be troub-le. The Sons of San-Gen - na - ro
Es gibt heu-te wie-der Är - ger. Die Bru-der-schaft San Gen-na - ro

p

M.C.

are all ex - cit - ed be - cause you won't take part in the pro - ces - sion. They
ist schon ganz aus - ser sich, weil du bei der Pro - zes-sion nicht mit gehst. Sie

M.C.

say: "We shall not have the pro-ces-sion with-out our lit-tle Saint!" They say
schrei'n: „Dass die klei - ne Heil'- ge nicht mit geht, kommt gar nicht in Be - tracht!" Sie schrei'n

f

M.C.

— that if Mi - che - le does-n't let you come, they'll drag you a - way by force.
wenn dich dein Bru-der heut nicht mit-gehn lässt, dann ho - len sie dich mit Ge-walt.

ff

Maria C.
M.C.
Annina
Ann.
Carmela
Car.
Assunta
A'ta
83
espr.
I'm
Ich
They must have all gone craz - y.
Die sind wohl nicht bei Tro - ste.
Ma-don-na San-ta. They must have all gone craz - y.
mf
not a - fraid. I must wait for him.
fürcht' mich nicht. Ich war - te hier.
You'd bet-ter hide. Don't let them
Bit - te ver - steck dich, dass sie dich nicht
espr.

M.C.
Ann.
Car.
A'ta
I'm on - ly a - fraid for him,
Ich fürch - te nur für ihn,
find you.
fin - den.
for Mi-che - le.
für Mi-che - le.
An- ni - na's right.
Sie hat ganz recht,
They all are
sie woll'n Mi -
I know those boys,
Die Brü-der kenn ich,

84
M.C.
af - - ter Mi - che - le.
che - le an den Kra - gen.
Ann.
Car.
rough-necks, hot-heads, bul-lies, and quick with knives.
Fle - gel, Strol-che, Row-dies mit lo - sen Mes-sern.
A'ta
Of all the days to
Aus-ge-rech-net
M.C.
Ann.
Where is he? Why
Wo ist er? Wo
Car.
Lis - ten, you had bet - ter stay right here.
Du bist nir-gends si - che - rer als hier.
A'ta
hap - pen! Yes, you'd bet - ter stay right
heu - te! Ja, am bes - ten bleibst du

M.C.
Ann.
does - n't he come?
kann er nur sein?
If
Wenn
Car.
Sure - ly San Gen - na - ro will pro - tect him.
Ihn wird San Gen - na - ro schon be - schüt - zen.
A'ta
here.
hier.
Don't you dare go out a -
Geh auf kei - nen Fall al -
M.C.
Some-one should go now and
Je - mand sollt' ihn war - nen, dass
Ann.
they will meet with him,
sie Mi - che - le fin - den,
Car.
No one will touch you if you're near us.
Dich rührt kei - ner an, wenn du hier bleibst.
A'ta
lone.
lein.
If you are anx - ious for Mi -
Wenn du dich um Mi - che - le

M.C.
tell him to stay a-way from the pro - ces - sion.
er sich heu-te am be - sten hier nicht sehn lässt.
Ann.
they will hurt him.
das wär schrek - lich.
Car.
If you're with him there will be troub - le.
Zu - sam-men darf man euch nicht se - hen.
(Assunta runs off.)
A'ta
che-le, I'll do my best to find him.
äng-stigst, dann wer-de ich ihn su - chen.
fff
(A group of noisy passersby are seen crossing the street.)
85
sff
sff
mf
Annina
Ann.
Saint Mi-chael, pro-tect him.
Sankt Mi - cha - el schütz ihn!
poco rall.
p
pp
ppp

86
Maria C.
(liberamente)
M.C.
Don't be a - fraid, An - ni - na,
Hab kei-ne Angst, An - ni - na,
I'll de-fend you with my
denn für dich tä - te ich
own life.
al - les.
You know, An - ni - na,
Du weisst, An - ni - na,
at first I did - n't be - lieve in
zu erst glaub - te ich nicht sehr an
you.
dich.
But since the day you touched my son,
Doch seit mein Sohn dich be - rührt hat,
he, who has - n't
fängt er an zu
spok - en since he was born, has be - gun to speak.
spre - chen, was er sein Le - ben lang nicht ge - konnt hat.
(turning to her boy)
(almost spoken)
Show An - ni - na.
Zeigs An - ni - na.
p

Maria C.
M.C.
Say: "Mam-ma, su bel-lo mio." Come on, say: "Mam-ma."
Sag „Mam ma, su bel-lo mio." Na wirds! Sag „Mam-ma."
Annina
Ann.
Oh, please!
Ich bitt' dich!
87
(Michele appears from the street and enters the lot.)
Boy (almost in a grunt)
Mam - ma
Mi - che-le, Mi-che-le!
Molto moderato e sostenuto
pp
p cresc.
Michele (to the women)
Mich.
I told you to leave my sis-ter a-lone.
Zum Teu-fel, lasst mei-ne Schwes-ter in Ruh.
mf

Ann.
Mich.
Oh, dear Mi-
Lie - ber Mi-
Stop hang-ing out here.
Was wollt ihr hier noch?
f
ff
88
(Carmela disappears into the house. Maria and her son hurry off
che-le!
che-le!
An - ni - na,
An - ni - na,
what has happened to you?
ja, was ist denn mit dir?
down the street.)
I am a -
Ich ha - be -
Why do you trem-ble so?
Und wa-rum zit-terst du?
mf
p

(liberamente)
Ann.
fraid.
Angst.
Why do you make peo-ple hate you so? Some day they'll harm you.
Wa-rum hast du dich so ver-hasst ge-macht? Wie soll das aus-gehn.
Mich.
What are you a-fraid of?
Ja, a-ber wo-vor denn?
I do not un-der-
Ich ver-ste-he es
But try to un-der-stand me. It's for your own sake.
Ver-stehst du mich denn gar nicht? Mir gehts um dein Wohl.
89
Andante
stand.
nicht.
I do not un-der-stand...
Ich ver-ste-he es nicht...
An-ni-na, you
An-ni-na du
pp
mf

Ann.
Yes, I know.
Ja, ich weiss.
Mich.
know how much I love you.
weisst, wie ich dich lie - be.
You know they all be -
Die Leu - te hal - ten
Ann.
Yes, I know.
Ja, ich weiss.
Mich.
lieve you are a saint.
dich für ei - ne Heil' - ge.
Look me in the eyes.
Sieh mich ein-mal an.
Ann.
Oh, no! I nev-er said that!
O nein! Das hab ich nie ge-sagt!
Mich.
Do you be-lieve your-self a saint?
Glaubst du, ei-ne Hei - li - ge zu sein?

Ann.
Mich.
Why, then do you let these peo-ple come to you, sick peo-ple,
Wa - rum er-laubst du dann, dass kran-ke Leu-te zu dir kom-men,
How can I help that?
Wie soll ich sie hin-dern.
(liberamente)
hop-ing to be cured?
da-mit du sie heilst?
Do you real-ly be-lieve that it is
Und glaubst du es wirk-lich, dass dir
90
poco meno
a tempo
Yes, — that I know.
Ja, — ganz ge-wiss.
Je-sus who ap-pears to you?
Je-sus er - schie-nen ist?
But you are ill and keep im-
Du bist doch krank, und stellst dir
mf

poco meno
Ann.
How can I im-ag-ine what is be-yond im-ag-in-ing?
Wie kann ich mir vor-stel-len, was völ-lig un-vor-stell bar ist?
Mich.
ag-in-ing things.
Din-ge oft vor.
a tempo
I do not ask to be be-lieved,
Ich will ja nicht, dass man mir glaubt,
rit.
But that is fool-ish, sense-less talk.
Wie du nur so tö-richt re-den kannst!
mf
rit.
91
Molto più mosso
but I be-lieve.
doch ich, ich glau-be.
Lis-ten, lis-ten care-ful-ly.
Schwes-ter, hör doch bit-te mal.
f
ff
Molto più mosso
f

(liberamente)
Mich.
You say that in Par-a-dise one eats gold-en bread. How can one "eat" gold?
Du sagst doch es gäb im Him-mel gol-de-nes Brot zu es-sen. Wer kann denn Gold es-sen?
Agitato
Ann.
I don't know... I don't claim to un-der - stand.
Dass weiss ich nicht... Ich ver-ste - he da-von nichts.
Mich.
Don't you see how
Sieh doch ein, wie
f
p calmo
92
Allegretto mosso
Ann
Stop tor-ment-ing me!
Bit - te, qüal mich nicht!
Mich.
child-ish it is?
kind-isch das ist.
Do you re-mem-ber, at school, how
Denk an die Schul-zeit zu-rück, da
Allegretto mosso
mf agitato

Mich.
chil-dren made fun of you be-cause you could-n't learn and how they used to call you
wur-dest du aus-ge-lacht, weil du nicht sehr be-gabt warst. Die Kin - der rie-fen im-mer
Ann
Yes,
Ja,
Mich.
"numb-skull, numb-skull?"
„Blö - de, Blö - de!"
ff
p
Ann
I re-mem-ber.
Ja, so war es.
(liberamente)
Mich.
Why, then, should God have cho-sen you, of all peo-ple?
Wa - rum hat Gott dann gra-de dich__ aus-er-wählt?
poco rit.
p

93
Un poco meno
affrettando
Ann.
Per - haps — be - cause I love Him.
Viel - leicht — weil ich Ihn lie - be.
Mich.
But
Doch
Un poco meno
p
mf
How else can I love Him since I am hu - man.
Wie sonst soll ich Ihn Lie - ben, wenn ich selbst ein Mensch bin.
Mich
you love God as if He were hu - man.
du liebst Gott, als ob Er ein Mensch wär.
f
f
How
Wie
But God is not a man.
A-ber Gott — ist kein Mensch.
He's ev-'ry-thing and noth-ing.
Er ist Al - les und Nichts.—
3
3

(94)

Ann.
can one de - sire ___ ev - 'ry - thing? Can one love ___ noth - ing? ___
könn-te man Al-les er - seh - nen? Kann man das Nichts ___ lie - ben? ___

Mich.

p *mf*

Ann
God I de - sire, ___ and that I know, ___ and
Gott er - sehn' ___ ich ein - zig, und Ihm ge -

Mich.

Ann
yearn ___ to be His bride. How long must I still
hö - - ren möcht ich gern. Wann ist es end-lich so -

Mich.

f

Ann
wait for that joy - ous meet - ing?
weit, dass Er als Braut mich an - nimmt?
Mich.
Nev-er, nev - er! You shall
Nie-mals, nie - mals! Du wirst
col canto
nev - er take the veil.
nie den Schlei-er neh-men
95
ff
God's will be done.
Was Gott will ge - schieht.
Sis - ter, I shall hide you and take you a - way,
Schwes - ter, ich ver - steck dich und bring dich hier fort,
Allegro moderato, ma con agitazione
pp

96
Ann
Mich
far — from these peo - ple, far from this street. Here the blood is dark-ened by
fort von die - sen Leu-ten wo nie-mand dich sieht.. Hier ist al - les dun - kel von
Ann.
Mich.
mem'- ries, and fears, me - dalled with i - dols, dag - gered by tears.
Trä - nen und Leid, trü - be von Furcht und Un - duld - sam - keit.
f
poco rit.
97
Ann
Mich
Here the young are brand - ed by a re - lent - less past,
Schon die Ju - gend trägt hier schwer an der Ver - gan - gen - heit,
a tempo
mp
f

Ann
Mich.
re - ceive its se - cret sig - nals, and bear the en - slav - ing
ist von Ge - burt ge - zeich - net und trägt schon das Skla - ven -
Ann.
Broth - er, I shall lead you and show you the way,
Bru - der, ich be - schütz' dich und zeig dir den Weg,
Mich.
mark.
mal.
p
Ann.
far from all fears, and far from the world.
fort von die - ser Welt, von Trä - nen und Leid.
Mich.

Ann.
In the Cit - y of God, love is con - stant and deep,
In der Stadt Uns-res Herrn wohnt nur Lie - be und Glück.
Mich.
f
Ann
poco rit.
joy with - out wine, and peace with - out
Wer sie be - tritt, sehnt sich nie mehr zu -
Mich.
poco rit.
98
a tempo
Ann.
sleep. All roads lead back to their be -
rück. Al - le We - ge füh ren uns im
Mich.
God can - not ev - er lose you, but you can be lost to
Gott kann dich nie ver-lie - ren, mir nur kannst du ver-lo - ren
a tempo

Ann.
gin - ing. An il - lu - sion is their goal.
Krei - se. Kei - ner führt uns an ein Ziel.

Mich.
me.
gehn.

(99)

Ann.
On - ly the road that leads to
Ei - ner al - lein führt gra - de -

Mich.
Don't ev er leave me. Los - ing you is
Bit - te, ver - lass mich nicht. Wenn ich dich ver -

Ann.
God is for - ev - er straight.
aus der Weg zu Gott, dem Herrn.

Mich.
los - ing all I have.
lie - re, hab ich gar nichts mehr.

rall.

100
a tempo
molto rall.
Ann
He who fights the ser - pent, will stand by your side.
Mi - cha - el, der Erz - en - gel, führt dich zu Ihm.
Mich.
I could nev - er live with - out you by my side.
Ich kann nicht mehr le - ben, wenn du mich ver - lässt.
f
molto rall.
ff
101
Allegretto, solenne
(All the arches above the street suddenly light up.)
Ann.
The pro-ces - sion is
Die Pro-zes-sion muss gleich
Chorus (off stage)
SOPRANO
Ve - glia su di noi
ALTO
TENOR
Ve - glia su di noi
BASS
Allegretto, solenne
pp
Tamburo

* Tamburo rhythm continues until Poco più mosso (Page 122)

Ann.
find me here _ there will be troub-le.
mich hier sehn, gibt's wie-der Är-ger.
Mi-
Mi-
Mich.
I'm not a-fraid of them._
Denkst du, ich fürch-te mich?
San - to d'ar - gen - - to.
San Gen-
San - to d'ar - gen - - to.
102
(A double row of barefoot women slowly passes by holding lighted candles. They are followed by
che - le.
che - le!
Let them come. Let them dare to touch you. They'll soon find
Soll ei-ner wa - gen, dich an-zu-rüh-ren! Dann soll'n sie
na - ro, San Gen - na - ro, San Gen -
Ve - - glia
Ve - - glia
cresc. poco a poco

men holding holy banners.)

Ann.
na - ro, pro-tect us! Ho - ly Vir - gin, Moth - er of
na - ro, be-schütz uns! Mut-ter Got-tes, hilf dei-nem

Mich.
A - lone a - gainst you all. ___
Ich steh al - lein ge-gen al - le.

na - ro, San Gen - na - ro, San Gen - na - - -

san - - to as - - -

san - - to as - - -

f

Ann.
God, have pit - y on me. Don't let an - y - thing hap-pen to Mi - che - le. Please, please.
Kind! Er - bar-me dich mein! Be-schüt-ze mei-nen Bru - der Mi - che - le! Bit-te, bit-te.

ro ___ splen - den - - te!

tro ___

tro ___ splen - den - - te!

103
Tu che pro - teg - gi la gen - te del mar gui - da - ci in
Tu che pro - teg - gi la gen - te del mar gui - da - ci in
por - to e non ci scor - dar. San Gen - na - ro, San Gen -
por - to e non ci scor - dar. Ve - -
104
dim. poco a poco

na - ro, San Gen - na - ro, San Gen - na - ro, San Gen - na - ro.
San Gen -
glia su di noi San - -
105
(The chorus is followed by a band which suddenly bursts into a march.)
Poco più mosso
na - ro.
to del san - gue!
Poco più mosso
BAND
Poco più mosso
ff secco

(At the same time, a group of young men stealthily enters the lot. While one of them holds Annina back, the others spring on Michele and hit him over the head. Michele falls to the ground, but quickly gets back on his feet and struggles with his assailants.)

(spoken)
Ann
Don't hurt him!
Lasst ihn los!
I'll come with you.
Ich komme mit euch.
Don't, don't...
Tut ihm nichts...
3
3

8
sff
sff

107
(Michele is overpowered and tied to the fence by his wrists. He is left hanging there, facing the audience. The young men then take hold of Annina, lift her to their shoulders and carry her outside, into the procession. The crowd cheers as she is slowly carried along, frightened and helpless.)
108
Mich.
An-ni - na, An-ni - na! Don't
An-ni - na, An-ni - na! An-
Tu che tut - to
Tu che tut - to
tempo primo subito
ff

Mich.
let them take you a-way.
ni-na, weh-re dich doch!
Ban-dits!
Narren!
Fa-nat-ics!
Ban-di-ten!
puoi.
Fac - ci la gra - zia
puoi.
Fac - ci la gra - zia
Mich
En-e-mies of God!
Das nennt sich Chri - - - - sten!
pre - - ga Ge - sù per noi.
pre - - ga Ge - sù per noi. San Gen-

109
(As Annina is carried off, a large, elaborate effigy of San Gennaro appears and slowly rolls by.)
San - to del do - lor.
na - ro, San Gen - na - ro, San Gen - na - ro, San Gen - na - ro, San Gen -
San - to del do - lor.
110
Mar - ti - re san - to sal - ga a te il
na - - ro san - to sal - ga a te il
Mar - ti - re

can - to del nos - tro cuor. Tie - ni lon -
can - to del nos - tro cuor. Tie - ni lon -
ta - no ma - lan - no e pian - to.
ta - no ma - lan - no e pian - to.

111
Ve - glia su di noi, San Gen-na - ro,
Ve - glia su di noi, San Gen-na -
San Gen-na-ro, San Gen-na-ro, San Gen-na-ro, San Gen-na-ro,
ro, San Gen-na - ro, San Gen-na - ro, San Gen-na - ro, San Gen-na -
dim. poco a poco

(As the last of the procession disappears, a few strollers are seen following it blowing paper trumpets and eating candies.)

p
(The Chorus continues in tempo (Allegro Solenne) regardless of orchestra tempo until the sign ⁂)
SOPRANO
113
pp lontano
San Gen-na - ro, San Gen-na - ro,
(off stage)
ALTO
pp lontano
pp
Desideria dressed in red with a carnation in her hair,
San Gen-na - - ro, San Gen-na - ro, etc.
(The Chorus continues in tempo (Allegro Solenne) regardless of orchestra tempo until the sign ⁂)
Andante sostenuto
poco rit.
p espr.

114

appears in the doorway, stage right. She stands there for a few seconds looking at ***Michele,***

then stealthily approaches him and unbinds him. As he breaks into loud sobbing, she kneels next

SOPRANO *(off stage)* *p*

Ve - glia

ALTO *p*

As before the chorus continues in the original tempo of the procession regardless of the orchestra tempi until the sign ✲

TENOR *p*

San Gen - na - ro, San Gen - na - ro, San Gen - na - ro, San Gen -

BASS *p*

Allegretto solenne come prima

pp

to him and passionately kisses him.)

Act Two

*(An Italian restaurant in the basement of a house on Bleecker Street. The ceiling is decorated with multi-colored paper chains and the walls are covered with frescoes depicting the Bay of Naples. Down stage right, an elaborate bar with a **caffè espresso machine**. Along the front of the stage, a few small tables with chairs. At the back of the restaurant, on a slight elevation, an empty area which evidently serves as the dance floor. **In one corner of it stands a huge** juke-box. Within this area, stage right, a door with a sign "Banquet Room"; stage left, another door leading to the kitchen. At the back of the stage, a third door which serves as the main entrance and a large, curtained window through which one can see the steps leading up to the street.*

*Facing the audience in smiling stillnes, Carmela, dressed as a bride, and Salvatore at her side, are having their photograph taken. **They are surrounded by relatives and guests, which include Annina, Michele, Assunta, Maria Corona and her son.**)*

Young Man
(spoken)
(parlato)
(laughter)
2
A'ta
way?
sehn!
Eh,
Kommt,
boys...
Kin-der...
Come on, let's
Wir wol-len
Young Man
dance.
tan - zen.
3

Subito moderato
(swing time) ♩= 128
(Everyone enters into the merriment of the occasion. A few couples dance while the remaining couples stand around and watch.)
Juke-Box
f
3
4
There nev - er was such a pair.
Das schön - ste Paar auf der Welt.
There. nev - er was such a pair.
Look at her
Mit sol- chem

hair, e-nough to make the neigh-bors die with en-vy.
Haar war es nicht schwer, sich ei-nen Mann zu ang-eln.
5
Look at his cheeks. Ah, what a sail-or his fa-ther must have
Ein schö-ner Mann! Er ist noch zwan-zig-mal hüb-scher als sein

(shouts and laughter)
been, to leave such blooms on those ol-ive cheeks!
Va-ter, der ein Mords-kerl von See-mann war.
Oh!
Oh!
They al-read-y knew in their moth-ers'
Sie war'n für ein-an-der be-stimmt, als
They al-read-y knew in their moth-ers'

wombs that they were meant to love each oth - er.
bei - de nach im Schoss der Müt - ter ruh - ten.
wombs that they were meant to love each oth - er.
6

(In spite of their protests, and among shouts of laughter, a very shy Carmela and a reluctant Salvatore are finally forced to dance together. One by one the other couples stop dancing and stand by to watch. The laughter and coarse jesting never ceases.)

7
There nev - er was such a pair.
Das schön - ste Paar auf der Welt.
There nev - er was such a pair.
Look how he
Sie zu um-
holds her; a - fraid of crush-ing her and, oh, so want-ing to.
fas - sen, fehlt ihm der Mut, und ge-rade das, das möcht' er doch.

Look how she clings to him; not e - ven dar - ing to look at him, a -
Sie sieht nicht auf zu ihm, denn sie be - fürch - tet, er könnt sie et - wa

fraid to tempt his lips and, oh, ___ so want-ing to.
küs-sen, da - bei möch-te sie grad das so gern.

(shouts and laughter)
8
Oh!
Oh!
Get go - ing, get go - ing! You ras - cal,
Macht wei-ter, macht wei-ter! So ein Fi -
Get go - ing, get go - ing! You ras - cal,

you, get go-ing, get go-ing! That's the way! You ras-cal,
lou, nur wei-ter, nur wei-ter! So ist's recht! So ein Fi-
you, get go-ing, get go-ing! That's the way! You ras-cal,
you, get go-ing, get go-ing, get go-ing! That's the way!
lou, nur wei-ter, nur wei-ter, nur wei-ter! So ist's recht!
you, get go-ing, get go-ing, get go-ing! That's the way!
poco rit.

9
(Wine is brought in. Everyone cheers.)
Primo tempo
corta
corta
ff
10
11

(A young man, wine glass in hand, jumps on a chair and toasts the bride.)
Hai
One Tenor
12
Lento a piacere
ff
a Tenor
l'oc - chio ne - ro, ne - ro del - la qua glia la cam - mi -
mf col canto
na - ta del - la tor - to - rel - - la. Chi ti
por - ta a l'al - ta - re non si sba - glia ch'io non ho vis - to

13
Allegro
(Another guest mounts a chair.)
a Tenor
mai spo-sa più bel - la.
One Baritone
a Bar.
Il
Ch'io non ho vis-to mai spo-sa più bel - la.
Ch'io non ho vis-to mai spo-sa più bel - la.
ff
Allegro
Lento, a piacere
gi - glio t'ha do-na-to la bian-chez - za. La ro - sa t'ha do -
mf col canto

poco rit.
a Bar.
na - to il suo co - lo - re. Chi ti spo - sa, Car - me - la può ben di -
re d'a - ve - re il pa - ra - di - so e non mo - ri - re.
14 Allegro
Michele (also jumping on a chair)
Mich.
Sei
D'a - ve - re il pa - ra - di - so e non mo - ri - re.
D'a - ve - re il pa - ra - di - so e non mo - ri - re.
Allegro
ff

Lento, a piacere
Mich
tut - ta bian - ca co - me il gel - so - mi - no. Hai l'oc - chio
f col canto
Mich.
dol - ce il pet - to pa - lom - bi - no. Chi ti
15
Mich.
ve - de pas - sar più non ri - po - sa e non ri -
Mich.
po - se - rà chi ti fa spo - sa.
16
(A huge wedding cake is brought in from the kitchen amid cheers.)
Allegro
ff

(The guests slowly walk into the "banquet room" where the wedding cake is being

brought. Carmela and Salvatore remain behind the crowd, talking to some of the guests.

Annina, almost hiding in a corner, front stage, looks tenderly at Carmela.)

Ann.
Car.
All that wine! It makes me gig-gle!
So-viel Wein! Ich bin ganz se-lig!
I don't know what I'm say-ing.
Und ich red nur noch Un-sinn.
How
Wie
love-ly you look! Just as I had im-ag-ined you!
hübsch siehst du aus! So hab ich dich mir vor-ge-stellt!
Sal-va-to-re, you come here, too.
Sal-va-to-re, Komm doch zu uns.
Salvatore
Sal.
Yes.
Ja.
(liberamente)
(nestling in Salvatore's arms)
(she giggles)
Look what I am marry-ing! Is-n't he fun-ny look-ing?
So sieht nun mein Mann aus! Ist er nicht ko-misch?

Ann.
You must not mind her. She does-n't
Sei ihr nicht bö - se. Sie meints nicht
Sal.
Car-me-la, be-have! Stop it, you sil-ly girl!
Car-me-la, be-nimm dich! Lass das! Sei nicht so al-bern!
19
mean it. She loves you ver-y much, you know.
so. Sie liebt dich sehr das weisst du doch.
I know, An-ni-na,
Ich weiss, An-ni-na,
(liberamente)
And you, Sal-va-to-re, will you make me a prom-ise?
Und du, Sal-va-to-re, ver-sprichst du mir et-was?
I know. Yes... Yes, An-ni-na.
ich weiss. Ja... Ja, An-ni-na.

20
Andantino, un poco mosso
Ann.
Be good to her, be kind. Of all my friends I love her
Sei lieb zu ihr und gut. Sie ist von al - len mir die
p
most. So gen-tle is her heart, so sweet and gay, and,
Lieb - ste. Sie hat ein zar-tes Herz voll Fröh-lich-keit... und
poco rit.
21
a tempo
yes,... a lit-tle sil-ly at times. Be good, be kind.
auch... von Zeit zu Zeit voll Tor-heit. Sei lieb und gut.
p
We were to take the veil to-geth-er, But here she is, all
Wir woll - ten bei-de den Schlei-er neh-men. Jetzt steht sie hier als
poco riten.
a tempo

Ann.
dressed in white, a diff-erent bride with a bright, red rose-bush in her heart
dei - ne Braut im an-dren Schlei-er. Ih-re Wan - gen glü - hen, Ro-sen gleich,
cresc.
poco rit.
fa tempo
22
(liberamente)
and bright, black stars in her eyes. She'll make you a good
ih-re Au - gen strah-len vor Glück. Sie wird ei-ne gu-te
p
poco rit.
wife, Sal-va-to-re. You'll see. Be good to her, be kind.
Eh - e-frau wer-den für dich. Sei lieb zu ihr und gut
pp dolciss.
poco rit.

(Hiding her tears, Carmela runs to Annina, who clasps her tenderly in her arms.)

(sound of cheering
from the banquet room)
poco meno mosso
25
(Desideria enters from the street entrance.)
Andante
26
secco
mf
Desideria
(liberamente)
Des.
Where is Mi-che-le?
Wo ist Mi-che-le?
Call him out,
Ruf ihn her,
Barman
(liberamente)
B'man
In there.
Da drin.

Des.
I want to speak to him.
ich möcht ihn spre - chen.
Why should I?
Wie - so denn?
B'man
You're not going to cause an-y troub-le, are you?
Du wirst uns doch kei - ne Ge-schich-ten ma-chen?
27
espr.
(After the barman has left, Desideria goes over to the bar and pours herself a drink, then paces nervously up and down, stopping at intervals, as if trying to pull herself together.)
p ma con intensità
f

28
ff
(Michele comes in from the banquet room and, on seeing Desideria, stops short.)
(liberamente)
(bitterly)
Des.
What in - deed!
Ra - te mal!
Mich.
(liberamente)
De - si - de - ria! What do you want in here?
De - si - de - ria! Was willst denn du hier?
ff
pp
6
3
More than the dev - il it - self, one fears the un - in - vit - ed guest.
Die un - ge - be - te - nen Gäs - te sind mei - stens nicht sehr be - liebt.
Why did you come, then?
Und wes - halb kommst du
f

29
Allegro moderato
Des.
My moth-er has turned me out of the house.
Weil mich mei-ne Mut-ter her-aus-ge-wor-fen hat.
My
Und mein
Mich.
Allegro moderato
p
lov-er's door is locked
Freund war nicht zu Haus,
(liberamente)
be-cause he's out sing-ing
weil er auf der Hoch-zeit
at oth-er girls' wed-dings.
von ei-ner an-dren ist.
30
Is this what you came here to tell me?
Und das sind dei-ne gan-zen Sor-gen?
a tempo
ff

Des.
Mich.
poco rit.
a tempo
Mi - che-le, Mi-che-le, try to un-der-stand. Of all the neigh-bors,
Mi - che-le, ver-such doch, mich zu ver-stehn. Von al-len Nach-barn
pp senza rit.
poco rit.
mf a tempo
I was the on-ly one not to be in-vit-ed. They call me a
bin ich als ein-zi-ge heu-te nicht ge-la-den. Sie schimp-fen mich
slut be-cause I sleep with you.
Hu - re, weil ich mit dir schla-fen-geh.
(liberamente)
I can no more be asked to christ-nings or
Kein Mensch lädt mich mehr ein zu ir-gend-wel-chen
f

31
Andante
Des.
wed-dings. But that does-n't keep you from going to them.
Fes - ten.. Doch dich hält das nicht ab, dort hin zu gehn.
Mich.
No, De-si-de-ria, not that.
Lass bit-te sol-che Re - den!
Andante
f
Don't you start try - ing to change me.
Auch du wirst mich nicht mehr än - dern.
No one,
Nie-mand,
p
espr.
not e-ven you, can rule o - ver my life. I must be free.
nicht ein-mal du, be - stimmt ü - ber mein Le - ben. Noch bin ich frei.
mf
p

Des.
Mich.
Let peo-ple love or hate me as they like, I shall not
Ob mich die Leu-te has-sen, ist mir gleich. Ich buh-le
f
mf
32
bar-gain for their choice.
nicht um ih-re Gunst.
(liberamente)
I nev-er asked you for your love.
Hab ich ver-langt, dass du mich liebst?
ff
Allegro
You of-fered it to me and, at the time, no price was men-tioned.
Du hast dich an-ge-bo-ten; von ei-nem Preis war nicht die Re-de.
mf secco
ff

Des.
How can you be so cruel,
Wie un-ge-recht du bist,
Mi - che - le.
Mi - che - le.
Mich.
poco rall.
mf
33
Allegro
Is it a ring I ask for?
Wollt' ich dich je-mals bin-den?
Or a white veil I hope for?
O-der zur Hei-rat zwin-gen?
I don't know.
Ich weiss nicht.
Allegro
Leave me a - lone.
Lass mich in Ruh.
All that I want is to be
Ich möch - te nur, dass du mir

34
Des.
Mich.
shown — how much you love me.
zeigst, — dass du mich lieb hast.
a tempo
Have-n't I sworn my love to you?
Hab ich's dir nicht ge - schwo - ren?
poco rit.
a tempo
Yes, you have.
Ja, das schon.
No, not that.
Nein, das nicht.
And have I been un - faith-ful?
War ich dir je-mals un-treu?
poco rit.
a tempo
poco rit.
What is it, then, that makes you doubt me?
Und wa - rum hast du dann noch Zwei - fel?
What will con-vince you?
Was soll ich noch tun?
f a tempo
fs

35
(desperately)
Des.
You're not a-shamed to love me!
Du sollst dich mei-ner nicht schä - men!
Mich.
But, De-si-de-ria,
A-ber, De-si-de-ria,
ff
p
(defiantly)
Then crown me with your pride
Dann steh auch ein für mich,
why should I be?
das tu ich doch nicht.
pp
mf appass.
36
and bind me with your love.
und steh zu dei-ner Lie - be.
It is all I ask.
Mehr ver-lang ich nicht.
f

Des.
Mich.
(liberamente)
If I ev-er felt that you, too, were a-shamed of me,
Wenn ich je-mals füh-le dass auch du mich ver-leug - nest,
ff
I'd kill my-self.
ver-gift ich mich.
But I love you, De-si-de-ria,
Ich lieb dich a-ber doch,
f
mf
and am proud of it.
und bin stolz dar-auf.
(Desideria and Michele look helplessly at each other. Then Michele gets himself a glass and a bottle of wine, sits at one of the tables and starts drinking.)
p
pp

Chorus (off-stage)
37 Andante calmo
SOPRANO
pp
Eh già _ gio-vi - not-ti vo-glion sta-re at-tor-no a - te; _ la
ALTO
pp
TENOR
Eh già _ gio-vi - not-ti vo-glion sta-re at-tor-no a - te; _ la
BASS
Andante calmo
ppp
lu - na splen-de di not-te, ma tu mia bel - la splen - di not - te e
lu - na splen-de di not-te, ma tu mia bel - la splen - di not - te e

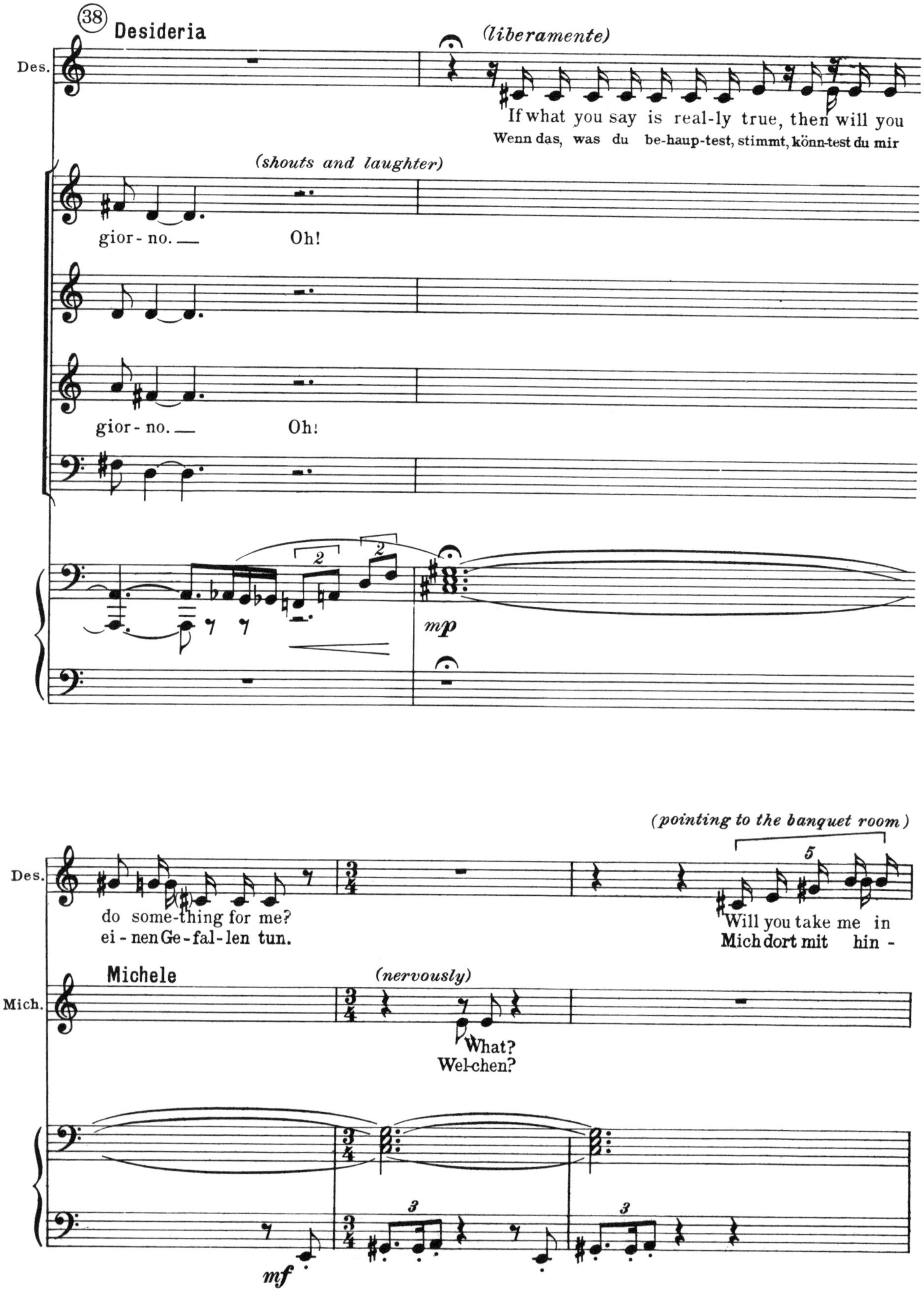

38 Desideria

Des.

(liberamente)

If what you say is real-ly true, then will you

Wenn das, was du be-haup-test, stimmt, könn-test du mir

(shouts and laughter)

gior - no. — Oh!

gior - no. — Oh!

mp

Des.
there with you?
ein - neh-men.
Why?
Wa - rum nicht?
(liberamente)
Mich.
That I can-not do.
Das ist nicht mö-glich.
You know why.
Ver- steh doch.
p
pp
Allegro
(she
An -
An -
Think of An-ni - na... Car-me-la is her best friend.
Denk an An-ni - na... Sie ist Car-me-las Freun - din.
Allegro
ff
39
springs toward him)
ni - na, An - ni - na, al - ways An - ni - na!
ni - na, An - ni - na, im - mer An - ni - na!

Des.
I knew it, I knew it! What does she ever do for you,
Dar-auf hab ich ge-war-tet! Was hat sie je ge-tan für dich,
f
sf>p
ex-cept light can-dles_ for your soul? But you are be-
als ein paar Ker-zen_für dich ge-weiht? Doch du bist be-
6
p cresc.
40
witched by her. You're ru-in-ing your life be-cause of her. Why
hext von ihr. Du zer-störst dein ganz-es Le-ben we-gen ihr. Wa-
ff
sfz p

Des.
don't you leave her a - lone?
rum lässt du sie nicht in Ruh?
She does - n't love you the way you think.
Sie liebt dich nicht so, wie du meinst.
She pit - ies you,
Sie be - mit - lei - det dich,
and you'll nev - er change her.
und du wirst sie nicht än - dern.
Nev - er,
Nie - mals,
nev - er, nev - er!
nie - mals, nie - mals!
41
She's like a blind - ed moth
Sie ist wie ein Schmet - ter - ling,
beat - ing her wings a - gainst a
wenn er, vom Licht ver - lockt, am
poco meno mosso
light - ed win - dow.
Fen - ster an - stösst.
In - fi - nite space is all a -
Un - zähl'ge Ster - ne stehn am

Des.
round her, but of the star - ry night she
Him - mel, doch von der gan - zen Pracht sieht
3
tr

Des.
3
on - ly sees — one lit - tle, flam - ing square.
sie nicht mehr — als ei - nen einz - 'gen Stern.
cresc.
tr

42
poco accel.
Des.
Why don't you let her go her way? Why don't you live with me? You
Lass sie doch gehn, wo-hin sie mag! Du hast doch mich da - für. Du
8
f
tr

(liberamente)
Andante
Des.
need me and you know it. You need me as much as I need you.
brauchst mich, und du weisst es. Du brauchst mich so sehr wie ich dich.
ff
43 sostenuto
I have but one love, and my love is not a blind dream.
Mei - ne Lie - be ist nicht schwär mer-isch und hei - lig,
My love blooms with the earth.
sie ist auf Er - den zu Haus.
(with exasperation)
Michele
Mich.
But what more do you want from me?
Hör doch end-lich mal auf da-mit.
p subito

44
Andante calmo
Michele
Mich.
There is noth-ing I can do a-bout An-ni-na. She's a
Über An-ni-na ist nichts wei-ter mehr zu sa-gen. Sie ist
Chorus (off-stage)
SOPRANO
E vo-la e vo-la il ven-to. Io mi strin-go ap-pres-so
ALTO
TENOR
E vo-la e vo-la il ven-to. Io mi strin-go ap-pres-so
BASS
Andante calmo
ppp
sick girl. She needs me.
kränk-lich. Sie braucht mich.
te. Il ven-to por-ta la piog-gia ma
p

45
Poco più mosso
Mich.
She's my sis-ter, af-ter all.
Je-der hilft doch sei-ner Schwes-ter.
(shouts and laughter)
tu Car-me-la fai la piog-gia e il so-le. Oh!
tu Car-me-la fai la piog-gia e il so-le. Oh!
Poco più mosso
cresc. poco a poco
Desideria
Des.
But she does-n't want to be your sis-ter.
Doch sie fühlt sich kei-nes-wegs als dei-ne Schwes-ter.
Des.
She wants to be ev-'ry-bo-dy's sis-ter.
Sie wä-re gern al-ler Leu-te Schwes-ter.

(liberamente)
(angry and defenseless)
Mich.
Stop talk-ing a-bout An-ni - na! She has noth-ing to do with us.
Lass end-lich An-ni - na in Frie-den! Sie hat gar nichts mit uns zu tun.
ff
(liberamente)
(with cruel persistence)
Des.
Well, then, will you take me in with you?
Al - so, nimmst du mich jetzt mit hin-ein?
mf
p
(Michele is silent)
Des
An-swer me.
Ant-wor - te!
rall.
pp
pp
46
Andante
Des.
Ah, Mi-che - le, don't you know that love can turn to
Ach, Mi-che - le, denk da - ran, die Lie - be wird zu
p
mf espr.

Des.
hate at the sound of one word, if the word is said too late?
Hass, wenn ein Wort, auf das man war - tet, un - aus - ge-spro - chen bleibt.
poco rit.
f
47
a tempo
Des.
Love can nev - er heal its wounds un - less the cry is
Lie - bes - wun - den hei - len nie, wenn der, der sie ge -
a tempo
sub. p
f
Des.
rit.
a tempo
an - swered, un - less the scar is seen.
schla - gen, die Wun - den gar nicht sieht.
a tempo
rit.
p
8

Poco più mosso
Des.
All the tears one weeps a - lone do not un - lock the
Al - le Trä - nen, die man ein - sam weint, er - lö - sen
8
poco rit.
a tempo
48
pound-ing gates of the heart. Like stars they fall
nie - mals das er-starr-te Herz. Sie fal - len wie Ster - ne
p
cresc. e rit.
in death-ly still-ness but leave — a poi-soned trail.
in To-des-stil - le, doch sicht bar bleibt ih - re Spur.
ff a tempo

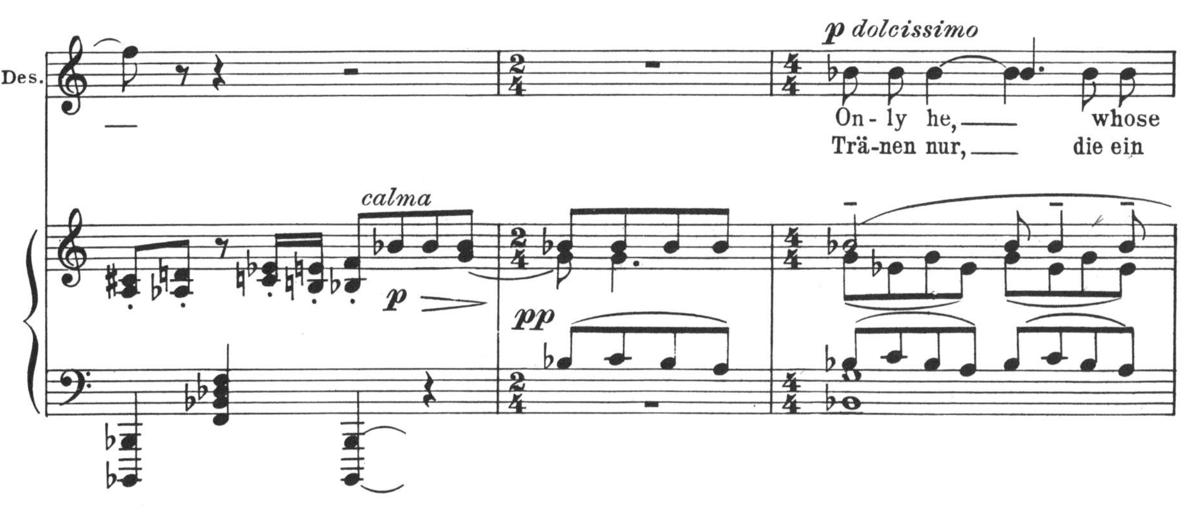
Des.
p dolcissimo
On - ly he, whose
Trä-nen nur, die ein
calma
p
pp

Des.
poco rit.
tears are mir - rored, can bear the se - cret pain of liv - ing.
an - drer mit weint, er - leich-tern Schmerz und Leid des Le - bens.
poco rit.

49
a tempo
Des.
Those of us, who find our love on earth, must cel - e - brate our fleet-ing
Al - le die, die sich in Lie - be fan - den, müs-sen ih - re Lie - be auch be -
a tempo
cresc.

Molto più mosso
Des.
tri - umph.
ken - nen.
Who wel-comes love in si-lence or hides it like a
Wer sei - ne Lie - be totschweigt, und Wer sich ih - rer
crime,
schämt,
shall soon run to the waste-lands to es-cape its blind-ing
soll fliehn, so-weit er flie - hen kann, sonst ver-fällt er ih - rer
50
ven - geance.
Ra - - che.
rall.

Des.
Ah, Mi-che-le,
Ach, Mi-che-le,
Tempo I°
ppp
mf dolce
don't for-get that love is a pit-i-less hunt-er when al-
glau-be mir, dass Lie - be mit dem To-de im Bun-de kein Er-
p cresc. molto espr.
51
a tempo
lied with death.
bar - men kennt.
f cresc. e rall.
6
ff
8

Andante moderato
Des.
(liberamente)
Mich.
You will re-gret it but if that is what you want, let's go
Du wirst's be-reu-en, a-ber bit-te wenn du willst, gehn wir
in. I'm not a-fraid of them.
rein. Mir soll es recht sein.
(He takes Desideria by the hand and leads her toward the banquet room, but at that same moment Don Marco appears at the door and bars the way.)
52
(4/4)
ff
I did.
Mit mir.
Don Marco (liberamente)
D.M.
5
De-si-de ria, who brought you here? You're not going to take her in there, are you?
De-si-de-ria, mit wem bist du hier? Sie soll doch nicht et-wa mit rein-kom-men?

Mich.
What bus-'ness is it of yours, Don Mar-co?
Geht Sie das et-was an, Don Mar - co?
D.M.
I beg you, Mi-che-le, don't an-tag-o -
Ich bitt Sie, Mi-che-le, pro-vo-zie-ren Sie
53
Allegro
(ironically)
I like that!
Zu gü - tig!
nize them a - gain, not to-day.... for your own sake.
sie heu - te nicht. Heu - te nicht... Um Ih-ret-wil-len.
Don't
Ich
Allegro
pp
For my own sake!
Um mei-net - wil - len!
I did not
Ich hab Sie
do it, Mi-che - le.
bitt Sie, Mi-che - le!
Take my ad - vice.
Ich mein es gut.
Don't take her in.
Sie darf nicht rein.

Mich.
ask you for your ad - vice.
nicht__ um Rat ge - fragt.
She's far a-bove an-y wo-man who's in
Sie ist tau-send-mal mehr wert als die Frau'n da
D. M.
sempre pp
54
there.
drin.
That may be so.
Das kann schon sein.
I do not pass judge-ment on her.
Je doch um das geht es hier nicht.
But I know___ that she will not be wel-comed there.
Ich weiss nur,___ dass man sie dort nicht ha - ben will.
p

55
Mich.
I don't care.
Ist mir gleich.
Let me pass.
Ich geh rein.
D. M.
I beg you,
Ich bitt Sie,
f
ff
p
poco cresc.
Mich.
D. M.
think it o-ver....
sei'n Sie fried-lich...
for An-ni-na's sake.
Scho-nen Sie An-ni - na.
mf
56
Don't you dare, priest,
Aus dem We - ge!
p
sff
Mich.
stand in my way.
Ich will rein - gehn.
Your ho-ly frock
Ihr schwar-zer Rock
does-n't fright-en me.
ist mir ei - ner - lei.
p
sff
p cresc.

Mich.
Ah,
Ah,
I warn you, get
ich war-ne Sie, ver-
ff
out of my way.
zie-hen Sie sich.
57
If you think I can be tamed by your mag-ic
Wenn Sie den-ken, dass mir Ihr Brim - bo - ri-um im-po-
p
signs,
niert,
you'll soon find out who Mi-che-le
dann täu - schen Hoch-wür - den sich a-ber
f

(He raises his fist at Don Marco, but he is held back by Annina, who has rushed out of the banquet room followed by the guests.)
Mich.
is!
sehr.
fff
58
Chorus
ALTO I
pp
It is Mi-che-le. De-si-de-ria is with
Es ist Mi-che-le. De-si-de-ria ist mit
ALTO II
pp
Mi-che-le, Mi-che-le,
BASS I
pp
Eh! What is the mat-ter? He's af-ter Don Mar-co a-
He! Was ist denn los hier? Er hat Streit mit Don Mar-co ge-
BASS II
pp
Who's hav-ing a fight? Mi-che-le, Mi-
Was ist hier für'n Krach? Mi-che-le, Mi-
f
p

Annina
Ann.
What is wrong, Mi-che-le?
Was ist los, Mi-che-le?
What have they done to you?
War-um er-regst du dich?
him, the lit-tle slut!
ihm, das Stras-sen-mensch!
Mi-che-le, Mi-che-le, Mi-che-le.
gain. One could have guessed it.
habt. Er kann's nicht las-sen.
che-le, Mi-che-le, Mi-che-le.
59 Andante
Salvatore
Sal.
(liberamente)
It is al-ways you, Mi-che-le, who caus-es troub-le.
Du brauchst nur wo-hin zu kom-men, schon geht der Krach los.
Why don't you
Lass uns doch
pp
mf

(Michele, who has pushed Annina away from him, pours himself a glass of wine, then, defiantly faces the hostile crowd.)
60
Lento
Sal.
leave us in peace? E-ven this day you had to spoil?
end-lich in Ruh! So-gar heu-te stän-kerst du rum.
p espr.
Michele
Mich.
I know that you all hate me. For you, I al-ways was the reb-el and the
Ich weiss, ihr al-le hasst mich. Ihr habt mich im-mer als Re-bell und Ket-zer
pp
p
curs-ed one. Since I was a child you've al-ways hat-ed me, be-cause I
an-ge-sehn. Als Kind habt ihr mich schon mit eurem Hass ver-folgt, weil ich nicht

Mich.
never asked for love, only under - standing. What
right have you to judge me? Look at your - selves! Al -
poco rall.
a tempo
Allegretto mosso e
p rall.
pp
62
agitato
though you made this land your home, you live like
pp
6

Mich.
stran - gers. You are a - shamed to
6
9
6
Mich.
say: "I was I - tal - ian."
9
6
9
63
Mich.
And for such lit - tle gain you sold your
6
9
9

Mich.
no - ble, an - - cient dreams.
leug - net eu - er Hei - mat - land.
6
12
10
poco rit.
a tempo
I can-not smile at your con - tent - ment, nor
Ich kann und will es nicht ver - ste - hen, dass
p
9
poco rit.
a tempo
64
share your lit - tle is - land of de - feat. I
dies arm - sel - ge Da - sein euch be - hagt. Denn
poco rit.
a tempo
do want to be - long, be - long to this new world. I
ich möcht hier zu Haus sein, in die - ser neu - en Welt. Ich
p
mf

Mich.
don't want to be told: "You foreigner, go back where you have
möchte nie mehr hören: "Du Fremder, geh nur dorthin, wo du
p
f
come from! You foreigner, go back to your old home."— My
herkommst! Du Fremder, geh zurück in deine Heimat!" Wo-
65
home... Where is my home? They tell me that the Italian
hin? In welche Heimat? Ich hörte, dass Italien
pp
mp
shore blooms like a garden. They tell me that no-
schön sei wie ein Garten. Und nirgends sei das
poco rubato
poco rubato

66
a tempo
Mich.
where the sea's so blue,
Meer so tief und blau.
that towns are built of
Die Städte ent-stam-men
stones old-er than sor - row,
sor-gen lo - sen Zei - ten
a tempo
mf
where men still live and
Die Men-schen dort sind
die, yes, ver-y poor but
arm, doch al-le frei und
f
proud.
stolz,
poco rall.
Per - haps if I could see just once that sad, sweet
Wenn ich das Land der Vä - ter ein - mal se - hen
67
Andante sostenuto
poco rall.
pp

Mich.
coun - try,
könn - te,
I would be proud to
viel-leicht wär ich dann
say: "I am I-tal - ian;"
gern ein I - ta-lie - ner
mf
cresc.
f
68
poco rit.
(grabbing a glass and throwing the wine in their faces)
and would for-get your
und säh euch nicht mehr
eyes.
an.
Take
Trinkt
your wine.
eu-ren Wein
al -
ff poco rit.
ff
(He collapses on a chair by a table and buries his head in his arms.)
69
(Some of the guests
Andante moderato
lein!
D.M.
You are wrong, Mi-
Du hast un-recht Mi-
Andante moderato
mf

file out of the restaurant, looking disdainfully at Michele as they pass him.)
D. M.
che-le.
che-le.
They are good peo-ple.
Sie sind gut - ar-tig.
You're a bit-ter man, Mi-
Und du bist ver-bit-tert, mein
p
mf
D. M.
che - le,
Freund.
and, a bit-ter man is a false judge.
Du hast kei-nen Grund, sie zu has - sen.
70
Annina
(sorrowfully to Carmela, lost and trembling in Salvatore's arms)
Ann.
I'm sor-ry, Car-me-la, I'm so a-shamed.
Ich schä-me mich Car-me-la, Es tut mir leid.
For-give him. It must be the wine.
Ver-zeih ihm. Er hat zu viel ge-trun-ken
p dolce
Ann.
Take her a-way, Sal-va-to-re, go on,
Bring sie nach Haus, Salvatore, bit-te.
We must not spoil your day.
Scha-de um das schö-ne Fest!
pp
mf

(Led by Don Marco, the bridal couple leaves, followed by relatives. As they mount the steps outside,
71
mp
leading onto the street, some of the guests who have been following, cheer lustily and throw rice at them.)
f
pp
(Only a few guests are now left in the room.)
Molto più mosso
p
f
(Annina approaches Michele and, for a moment, stands by him without moving.)
mf
f
ff
mf secco
rall.
72
Annina
(timidly caressing his head)
Adagio
Ann.
Mi - che-le.
Michele
(gratefully looks up at her)
5
Mich.
For-give me, An-ni-na.
Ver-zeih mir, An-ni-na.
Adagio
p
mf

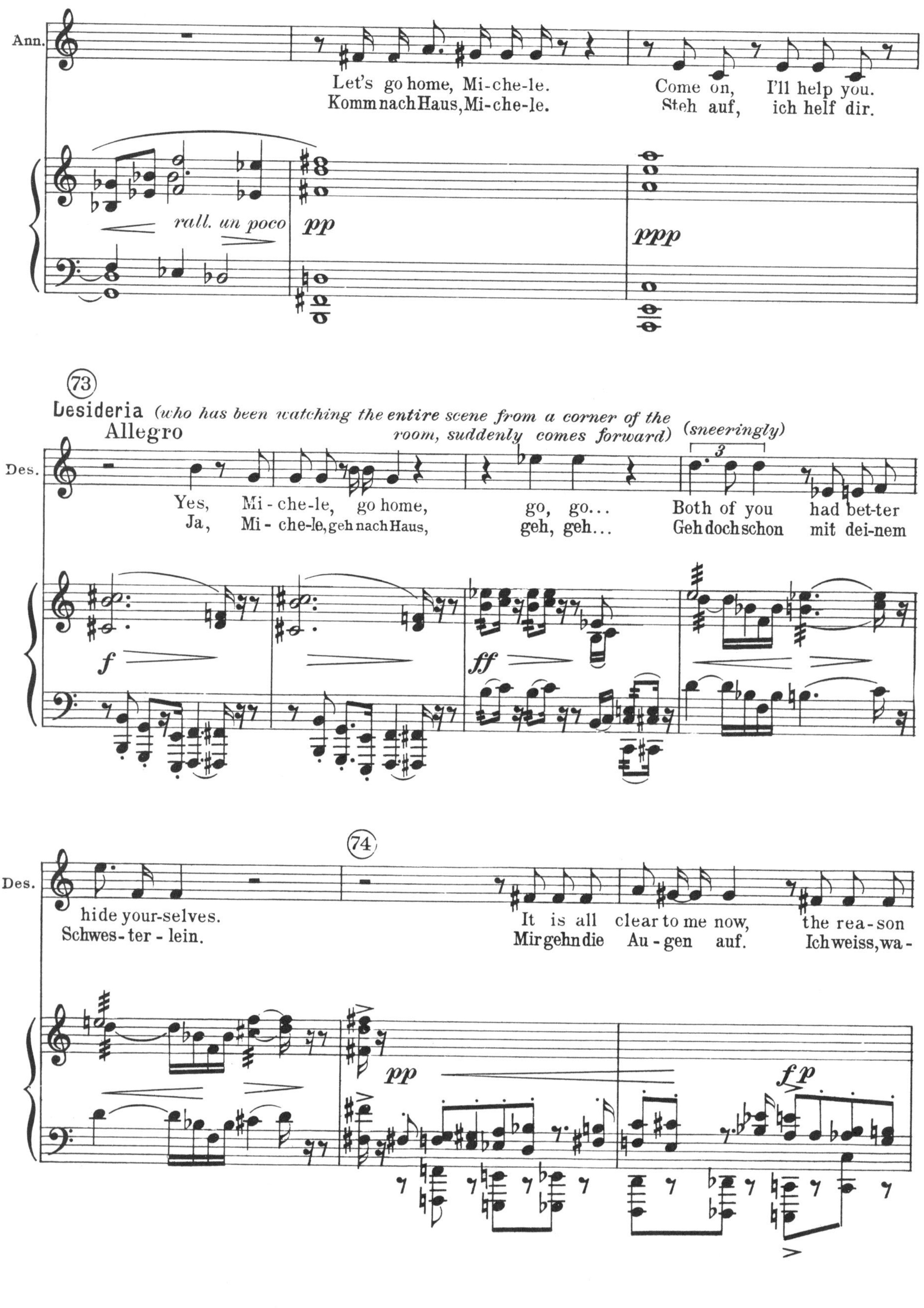

73

Desideria (who has been watching the entire scene from a corner of the room, suddenly comes forward)

Allegro

(sneeringly)

Des.

Yes, Mi-che-le, go home, go, go... Both of you had bet-ter

Ja, Mi-che-le, geh nach Haus, geh, geh... Geh doch schon mit dei-nem

f

ff

Des.

74

hide your-selves. It is all clear to me now, the rea-son

Schwes-ter-lein. Mir gehn die Au-gen auf. Ich weiss, wa-

pp

fp

Des.
why you will not mar - ry me. It is not I who should be a-shamed,
rum du mich nicht hei - ra - test, und dass es an mir ganz si-cher nicht liegt,
5
f p
f p
Des.
be - cause my love is bright - er than the sun,
denn mei - ne Lie - - be muss sich nicht ver - stek - ken
f p
f p
75
Des.
but you... but you... you...
A-ber du... a - ber du... du...
p
f

(liberamente)
(pointing at Annina)
Des.
Let ev-'ry-one hear this. It is not with me that you're in love, it is with her.
Jetzt soll's je-der wis-sen: Du warst nie in mich ver-liebt, son-dern in sie,
ff
76
Andante
Des.
it is with her.
in sie, in sie.
Michele
Mich.
(Michele looks stunned, as if he had been struck.)
What did you say?
Sag das noch mal.
Andante
ff
pp
77
Allegro
(as if possessed)
Des.
Yes, it is true... and she knows it.
Then freeing himself from Annina, he slowly moves toward Desideria.)
Das ist die Wahr - heit, und sie weiss es.
Mich.
Allegro
p
p

Annina (pulling him back)
Ann.
Come, Mi - che-le, leave her a - lone.
Komm, Mi - che-le, lass sie in Ruh.
Des.
Oh, the lit - tle
Ach, die klei-ne
Mich.
It is a lie, it is a lie!
Es ist ge-lo-gen, es ist ge-lo-gen
mf secco
p
f
Des.
saint, steal-ing her broth-er's heart.
Heil' - ge und ihr Brü - der - chen!
78
(spoken)
Mich.
You bitch!
Du Hure!
sff
pp subito

Des.
Mich.
(advancing menacingly toward Desideria)
Shut up! Don't dare say an-y-thing a - bout my sis - ter.
Halt's Maul! Kein Wort mehr ü - ber mei - ne Schwes-ter.
secco
cresc.
You are a - fraid
Du kannst die Wahr -
You street walk-er!
Du Drecks-hu - re,
You liar!
ver - lo-ge-ne!
f
p
to hear the truth!
heit nicht er - tra - gen
79
Nev - er!
Nein!
Nev - er!
Nein!
Take it back!
Halt dein Maul!
Take it back!
Halt dein Maul!

Annina
Ann.
Come home, Mi-che-le, you're drunk!
Wir ge-hen lie-ber, komm mit!
(Desideria laughs hysterically as Michele shakes her by the shoulders.)
Mich.
Don't joke with me!
Ich war-ne dich!
TENOR
Don't both - er with her.
Sie meint es nicht so.
BASSES
p
Leave her a - lone, Mi - che - le. Don't
Lass sie in Ruh', Mi - che - le. Sie
sf
p cresc.
sf
sf
80
Please stop him!
Komm, bit - te!
Mi-che - le,
Mi-che - le,
Mi-che - le,
Mi-che - le,
Ah, De-si - de-ria, de - ny what you
Ah, De-si - de-ria, das nimmst du zu -
both - er with her.
meint es nicht so.
mf espr.

Ann.
Des.
Mich.
Let's go, Mi-che-le,
Be-ruh-ige dich,
It's true,
Nein, nein!
it's true!
Nein, nein!
said.
rück.
I warn you, De-si - de - ria, you'll
Ich warn dich, De-si - de - ria, gib
p
simile
81
leave her a-lone.
du bist be-trunken.
Ad-mit it,
Ich lüg nicht,
ad-mit it!
ich lüg nicht!
pay for your lies!
zu, dass du lügst!
Ah,
Nimm
come prima
simile
ff

Ann.
You must not lis-ten to her, Mi-che-le.
Ich bitt dich, hörnichtaufsie, Mi-che-le.
Des.
Mich.
for your own sake, take back your
dich in acht! Zum letz ten
82
(more and more defiantly and hysterically)
Des.
You love her, you love her, you
Du liebst sie, du liebst sie du
(slowly cornering Desideria against the bar)
Mich.
words.
Mal!
(spoken:) Take it back! Take it back!
(gesprochen:) Nimm das zurück! Nimm das zurück!
f
ff

Des.
love her!
Liebst sie!
It's true, You
Ich weiss, du
love her,
liebst sie,
you
du
Mich.
Take it back, I said!
Nimm das zurück, sag ich dir!
Shut up!
Schweig!
(Michele, his body pressed against hers, suddenly seizes a knife from the bar, and stabs Desideria in the back. Everyone stands frozen-still.)
83
Des.
love her,
liebst sie.
you love her, love her!
Ich weiss, du liebst sie!
Mich.
Shut up!
Schweig!
Andante sostenuto,
fff
quasi adagio
(Having pushed Michele away from her, Desideria takes a few steps forward, then stands still again, her eyes wide open as if she were searching for something.)
3
affrettando

(She advances another step, trying with one arm to reach the wound in her back.)
84
affrettando
Annina (running to her side)
Ann.
De-si-de-ria,
De-si-de-ria,
De-si-de-ria!
De-si-de-ria!
Oh, my God, my
Oh, mein Gott mein
Desideria (Desideria suddenly collapses. A few women scream.)
Des.
più mosso
85
(The barman runs to a telephone booth to call the police.)
God!
Gott!
An-ni-na,
An-ni-na,
I'm dy-ing...
ich ster-be...
p subito

(Michele, as if suddenly waking from a dream, runs out of the restaurant, knocking a table down as he does so.)
(After he leaves, the few remaining guests stand against the exit door, and watch the following scene from there.)
Des.
For-
Ver-
f
8
(The stairway outside slowly becomes crowded with people, peering through the door and the windows.)
86
Ann.
(holding Desideria in her arms)
No, don't
Sag das
Des.
give me, An-ni-na. Help me, I'm dy - ing...
zeih mir, An-ni-na. Hilf mir, ich ster - be...
sempre p
f subito
Ann.
say that. It is-n't true, De-si-de-ria, it is-n't true!
nicht. Du wirst le - ben, De - si - de - ria, ganz ge-wiss!

(87)

Ann.

Des.
I'm a - fraid. An - ni - na, help me...
Ich hab Angst, An - ni - na, hilf mir.

pp f pp

3

Ann.
Don't be a-fraid, De-si-de-ria, don't be a-fraid. Pray with me.
Ängst'ge dich nicht, De-si-de-ria, ängst'ge dich nicht, Bet mit mir.

7 3 3

Des.
Yes,
Ja,

Adagio ma non troppo

f ppp

3

(88)

Ann.
O, mer - ci-ful God,
Barm - her - zi-ger Gott,

3

Des.
yes... O, mer-ci-ful God...
ja... Barm-her-zi-ger Gott...

pp

3

ppp

Ann.
Have pit - y on me
er - bar-me dich mein,
for I have suf-fered much.
denn ich hab viel ge-lit - ten.
Des.
Have pit-y on me...
Er-bar-me dich mein...
89
Allegro molto agitato
(suddenly clutching at Annina, terror in her voice)
An - ni - na, An-ni-na! I am a-fraid I'm dy-ing...
An - ni - na, An-ni-na! Ich hab so Angst', ich ster-be...
Allegro molto agitato
p
mf
f
(She slowly calms down, while Annina caresses her cheeks.)
90
Adagio ma non troppo come prima
Lead me, O Lord,
Nimm mich, o Herr,
Help me, help me!
Hilf mir, hilf mir!
Lead me, O Lord...
Nimm mich o Herr...
Adagio ma non troppo come prima
ff
pp

Ann.
To Your joy ful King dom,
in den Him - mel auf,
Des.
joy-ful... King-dom
in den Him-mel...
91
where I may find my peace
wo ich den Frie - den fin - de
in Your In-fi-nite
in Dei-ner un-end-li-chen
find.. my peace...
Frie - den fin-de...
love... Lie - be...
(in a murmer)
(Desideria dies.)
love... love... love...
Lie-be... Lie-be... Lie-be...
pppp
p

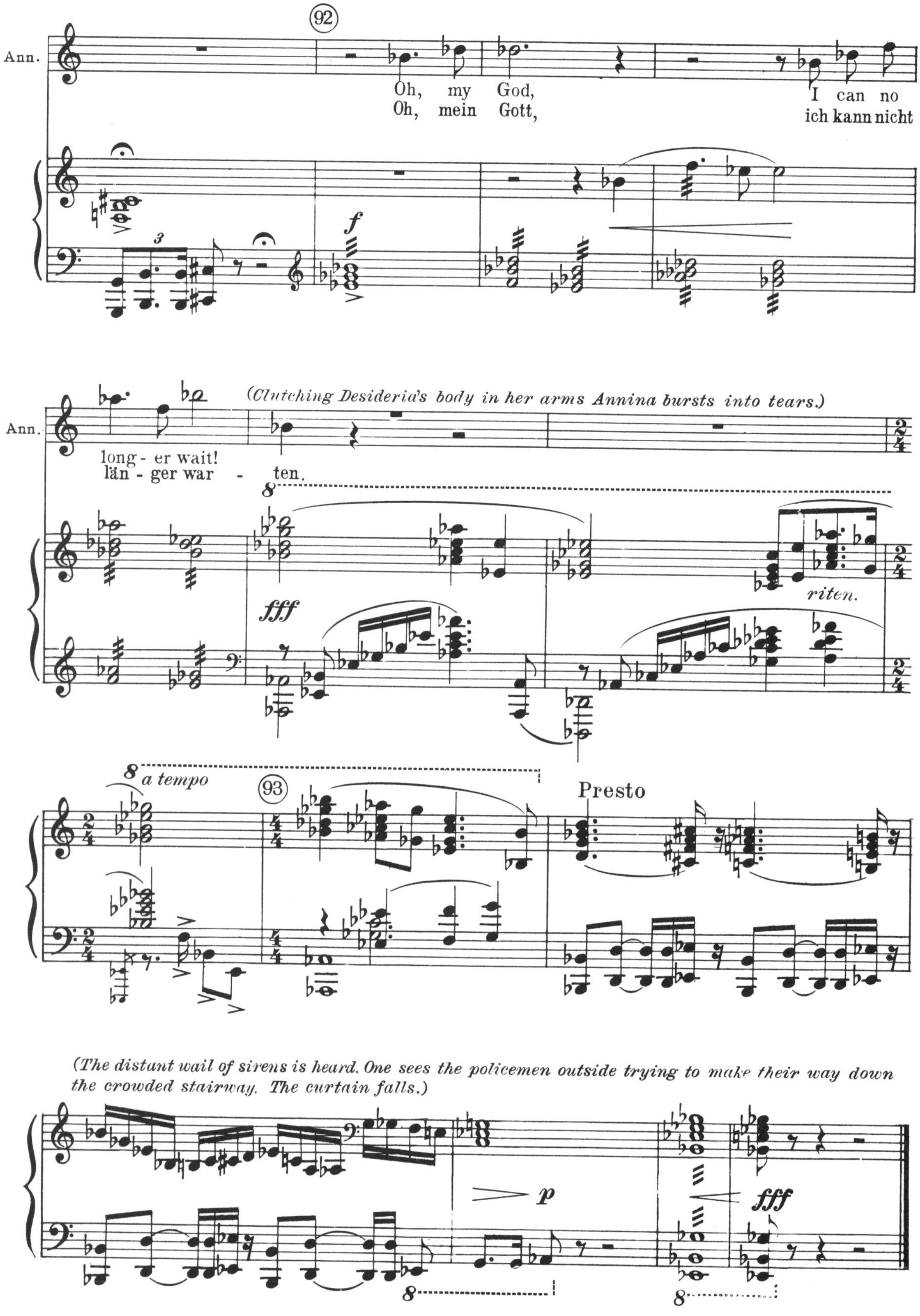

Ann.

(Clutching Desideria's body in her arms Annina bursts into tears.)

long - er wait!
län - ger war - ten.

fff

riten.

a tempo

93

Presto

(The distant wail of sirens is heard. One sees the policemen outside trying to make their way down the crowded stairway. The curtain falls.)

Act Three
Scene I

(A vast, dimly-lit, deserted passageway in a subway station. Upstage, a stairway leading to the street. Stage left, a newspaper kiosk, the interior of which is open to the audience. Stage right, an iron railing with a high, spoked turnstile which marks the exit from the subway station proper; behind the railing, a stairway leading up from the train level below. It is early morning. Blown by the wind, snow is piling high on the steps leading up to the barely visible street. The damp walls and the floor, littered with discarded newspapers, heighten the desolate atmosphere. Only the interior of the kiosk, warmed by an oil stove and lit by a little, electric lamp, is faintly cheerful. At rare intervals throughout the scene (specifically after the rumble of passing trains heard below) a few, chilled passengers will be seen emerging from the stairwell leading up from the station, coming through the turnstile, and disappearing up the stairway leading to the street.

As the curtain rises, Annina, wrapped in a shawl, is standing near the street exit, nervously waiting for someone. Maria Corona, while keeping an anxious eye on Annina, bundles up her son and sends him off with the morning papers under his arms.)

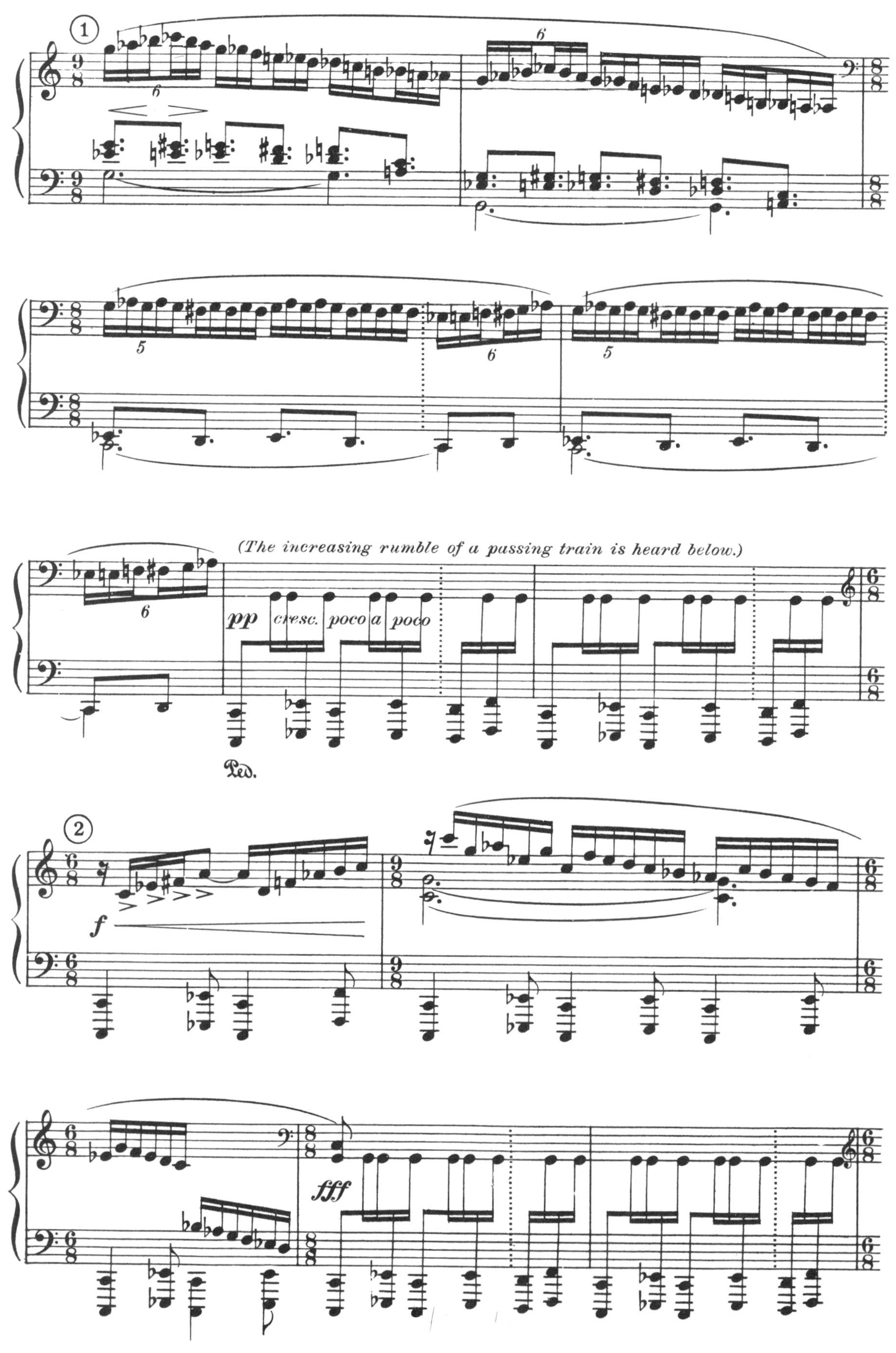
1
6
6
5
6
5
6
(The increasing rumble of a passing train is heard below.)
pp
cresc.
poco
a
poco
Ped.
2
f
fff

3
ff
(The noise of the train quickly dies away.)
mp
5
pp
6
5
6

4
pppp
morendo
Allegretto (liberamente)
Maria C. (going toward Annina)
M.C.
Stop wor-ry-ing, An-ni - na. He's sure to come. Don Mar - co won't be -
Be - ruh'-ge dich, An-ni - na. Er kommt schon noch. Don Mar - co wird ihm
mf secco
mf
tray him be - cause Mi-che - le asked for his help at the con-fes-sion-al.
hel - fen. Er hat's Mi-che - le hei - lig ver spro-chen, als er ge-beich-tet hat.
It is still ear - ly. Come and sit in - side.
Es ist noch früh. Komm zu mir her ein.
p

5
M.C.
Oh, poor lit-tle an - gel, come here and sit next to me.
Oh, du ar-mer En - gel, komm doch und setz dich zu mir.
rall.
Andante
(liberamente)
It is-n't quite sev-en yet.
Nochnicht ein-mal sie - ben.
Annina
Ann.
What time is it?
Wie spät ist es?
pp
The day is just be-gin-ning.
Der Tag fängt grad erst an.
It's damp down here.
's ist feucht hier un-ten.

6 Allegretto
(leading Annina inside the kiosk)
(they sit by the stove.)
M.C.
Come in-side. It's nice and warm in here. Is-n't this cheer-ful?
Komm doch schon. 's ist ganz schön warm hierdrin. Ist doch ge-müt-lich!
Ann.
Allegretto
p
f p
This is my home. Oh, poor an-gel, you look so tired.
Das ist mein Heim. Ar-mer En-gel, du siehst so müd aus.
pp
p
(liberamente)
(showing Annina an old newspaper)
5
Did you see Mi-che-le's pic-ture in the I-tal-ian pa-pers? Right on the front page,
Hast du mal Mi-che-les Bild in den Zei-tun-gen ge sehn? Auf der ers-ten Sei-te,

M.C.
as big as life! Oh, what a good-look-ing boy he is. I kept them all. Lis-ten to this:
in Le-bens grösse! Sieht er nicht wirk-lich sehr gut aus? Ich hab sie al-le. Die hier zum Bei-spiel:
Ann.
7
(quasi parlato)
"Un im-pres-sio - nan - te tra - ge - dia ha a - vu - to luo - go ier
se - ra..."
No, please. Don't read it. Don't let me hear it.
Bit - te! Nein, lass es. Ich kann das nicht hö - ren.

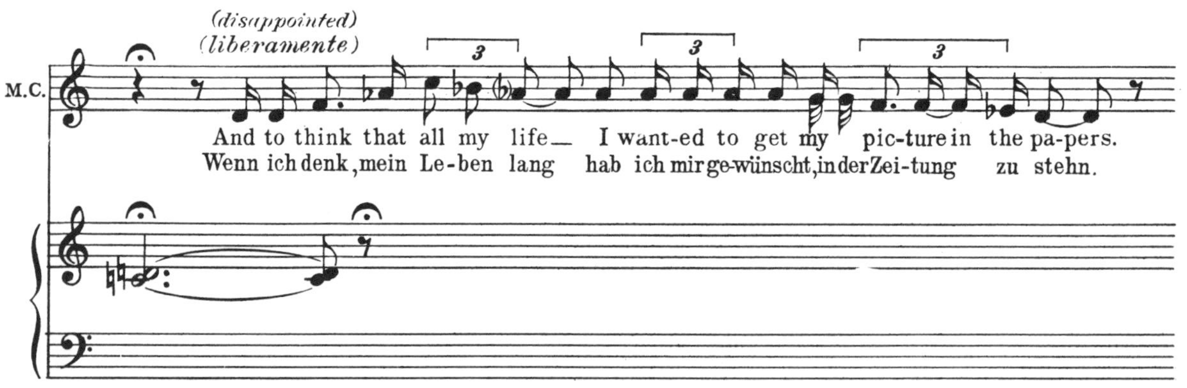
(disappointed)
(liberamente)
M.C.
And to think that all my life_ I want-ed to get my pic-ture in the pa-pers.
Wenn ich denk, mein Le-ben lang hab ich mir ge-wünscht, in der Zei-tung zu stehn.

M.C.
For twen-ty-five years I've been sell-ing this trash and not once have I been men-tioned in it.
Seit fünf-und-zwan-zig Ja-hren_ ver-kauf ich den Dreck, und nicht ein-mal war ich sel-ber_ drin.

8 - 11
(pulling some old newspaper clippings out of a drawer)
M.C.
Some peo-ple have all the luck.
Ja manch ei-ner hat halt Pech.
You re-
Das war
pp

M.C.
mem-ber the time Ma-ri-nel-la stabbed her sis-ter-in-law twen-ty times with a rust-y, kit-chen
auch so ein Fall, als Ma-ri-nel-la ih-re Schwä-ge-rin zwan-zig-mal min-de-stens mit ei-nem Mes-ser
pp
12
knife. (Her name was Cla-ra.)
stach. Sie hiess Cla-ra.
The poor girl bled for sev-en days and al-most lost her life.
Sie blu-te-te sechs Ta-ge lang und war so gut wie hin.
But all the re-port-ers took Ma-ri-nel-la's pho-to-graph in a bath-ing suit,
Da-für a-ber wur-de ein Bild von ihr im Ba-de-an-zug ab-ge-druckt,

poco rall.
13
a tempo
M.C.
all bathed in tears.
ge - ba-det in Trä-nen,
And can you im-ag-ine
Und kannst du dir vor-stell'n,
what they print-ed un-der it
was als Ü - ber-schrift da rü - ber
f a tempo
all?
stand.
(melodramatically)
"Pro - ta - go - ni - sta d'un dram-ma
di ge-lo - si - a."
14
But I am old and ug - ly and
Doch ich bin alt und häss - lich, und
p
no one takes my pic-ture.
nichts mehr für Re - por - ter.
(liberamente)
I guess I'll have to kill some-bod-y to have my pic-ture tak-en.
Ich müss-te ei-nen Mord be - gehn, sonst bringt kein Mensch mein Bild.
mf

(The rumble of a train is heard again. Annina, exhausted from her long wait, dozes off, her head leaning against Maria Corona's shoulder.)

(Don Marco comes down the street stairway.)

(After looking around him, he goes back and redescends, immediately followed by Michele.)

17
pp
morendo
Andante
D.M.
Don Marco
(liberamente)
There she is. Be care-ful, Mi-che-le, try_ not to up-set her.
Da drin ist sie. Ich bitt Sie, Mi-che-le, scho-nen Sie die Ar-me.
pp
Poco meno
18
Re-mem-ber, she's a ver-y sick girl. May God for-give you.
Be-den-ken Sie, sie ist wirk-lich sehr krank. Gott sei mit Ih - nen.
p
mp
(Don Marco quickly remounts the steps and disappears.)
May God_ for-give us all.
Und Gott sei mit uns al-len.

19
Andante molto moderato
(Evidently in great anguish and unable to control himself, Michele leans against the wall, covering his face with his hands.)
ppp
mf
p
Maria C.
M.C.
(tapping her on the shoulder)
I think he's here, An-ni-na.
Er ist jetzt da, An-ní-na.
Annina
Ann.
Where?
Wo?
f
(running to him)
Mi-che-le, Mi-che-le!
20
Allegro
Michele
accelerando
Mich.
An-ni-na, An-ni-na,
Allegro

(They clasp each other in an intense embrace.)
Ann.
Mich.
My An-ni - na!
ach, An-ni - na!
accelerando
21
Presto
Presto
poco rall.
mf
22
Allegro
How are you, Mi - che - le? Where are you hid - ing?
Wie gehts dir, Mi - che - le? Wo warst du ver - bor - gen?
Allegro
p

(Annina leads Michele to a little, wooden bench outside the kiosk.)
Ann.
Mich.
Ev-'ry-where. There will be no more peace for me.
Frag mich nicht. Für mich gibts kei-nen Frie-den mehr.
Give your-self
Stell dich end-lich
pp
23
up, Mi-che-le. You must ac-cept your pun-ish-ment.
selbst, Mi-che-le. Du musst dei-ne Stra-fe an-neh-men.
Nev-er.
Nie-mals.
f
Don't ask me to do that.
Ver-lang das nicht von mir.
(liberamente)
E-ven if God him-self be a-gainst me,
Und wenn Gott sel-ber ge-gen mich wä-re,
ff

24
Ann.
Mich.
I'll fight on to the end.
ich kämp-fe bis zum En-de.
ppp
pp
25
Andante
(with sudden hopelessness)
Where are my hopes and my
In ei - ner ein - zi - gen
ppp morendo
rit.
Andante
pp
dreams? With-in a sin-gle hour, all was lost, all was gone.
Stun - de ist auch die klein-ste Hoff - nung für im - mer ent - schwun -
poco accel.
a tempo

26
Mich.
den.
In that one glass of bit-ter wine, my
Durch ein paar Glä-ser schlechten Wein ist mein
pp
Ann.
Ah, poor Mi-che-le, where will you
Ar-mer Mi-che-le, was wirst du
Mich.
whole life was drowned.
Le-ben zer-stört.
p
cresc.
Ann.
go? Your night will have no dark-ness, no com-pass your
tun? Dir gibt die Nacht kein Dun-kel dir gibt der Tag kein
Mich.
My night will have no dark-ness, no com-pass my
Mir gibt die Nacht kein Dun-kel mir gibt der Tag kein
poco accel.
f
rall.
8

27
poco più mosso
poco rit.
Ann.
flight.
Ziel.
Mich.
flight.
Ziel.
On ly you are left to
Du bist al - les, was mir
pp dolcissimo
poco rit.
Ann.
Mich.
me, An - ni - na, you, my sis - ter,
blieb, An - ni - na. mei - ne Schwes-ter,
Ann.
Mich.
you, my gen - tle light.
du, mein Le - - bens licht. Für

28
Ann.
Mich.
I must fight on for you.
Oh, my
ff
God, please help me to find the strength to
29
tell him.
What must you tell me?
What is it, An-ni-na?
mf espr.

poco rit.
Meno mosso
Ann.
I'm ill, Mi - che - le, ver - y ill.
Mich.
poco rit.
Meno mosso
p
pp
Ann.
I'm going to die ver - y soon. My
Mich.
Who told you?
Poco più mosso
Ann.
"voi - ces" have told me and my "voi - ces" nev - er lie.
Mich.
You're
Poco più mosso

Mich.
wrong, An - ni - na, your "voi - ces" are your on - ly
mp
3
3

allargando un poco
Mich.
ill - ness and they can al - ways lie.
allargando un poco
3
f

a tempo
rall.
Andante mod.
Mich.
For-get them, for-get them!
a tempo
rall.
Andante mod.
p
pp

32
Ann.
Don't try to stop me, Mi - che-le.
Du kannst nichts än-dern, Mi - che-le.
Tell me good-bye, Mi-che-le.
Sag mir Leb-wohl,
Mich.
p
33
Più agitato
I'm going to take the veil.
Ich neh - me den Schleier.
(half-spoken)
(quasi parlato)
What do you mean?
Was soll das heis-sen?
No! No! I'll
Nein! Nein! Nein,
Più agitato
p cresc.
nev - er con - sent to that. How
das er - laub ich nicht. Das
can you e-ven think of it! No!
kann doch wohl dein Ernst nicht sein! Nein!
f
ff

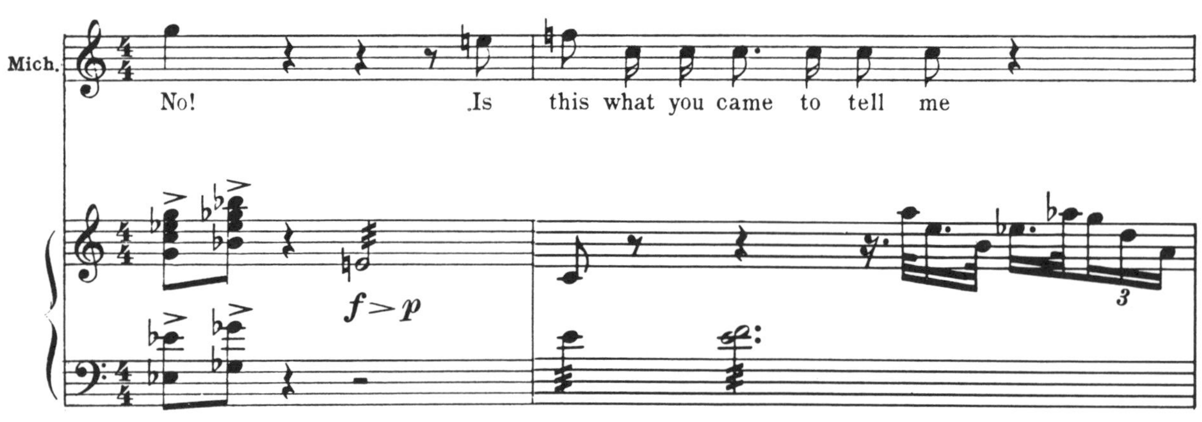
Mich.
No! Is this what you came to tell me
f > p
3

Mich.
now that I need you most.

34
Mich.
No! No! You can-not do that to me. I won't let you.
3
ff

(liberamente)
Mich.
What good are you to the world, if you can let down your own broth-er as he cries for
Wo - zu bist du auf die-ser Welt, wenn du dei-nen Bru-der im Stich lässt, wenn er Hil - fe
35
(scanning a magazine of horoscopes, inside the kiosk)
Maria C.
M.C.
Weep - ing, these, for him, are days of
Trä - nen. Die - se Ta - ge brin-gen
(Feeling himself watched by a couple of passengers walking down the platform, Michele walks to a dark corner, and nervously lights a cigarette.)
Mich.
help.
braucht!
ff
pp dolce
M.C.
weep - ing. It is all pre - dict - ed clear - ly in his sky.
Trä - nen. Das steht al - les klar in sei - nem Ho - ro - skop.

M.C.
Ve - nus has moved in - to the
M.C.
sun - house of Cap - ri - corn.
Ah,
pp
poco rall.
M.C.
me, for an - y man born in Ju -
poco rall.

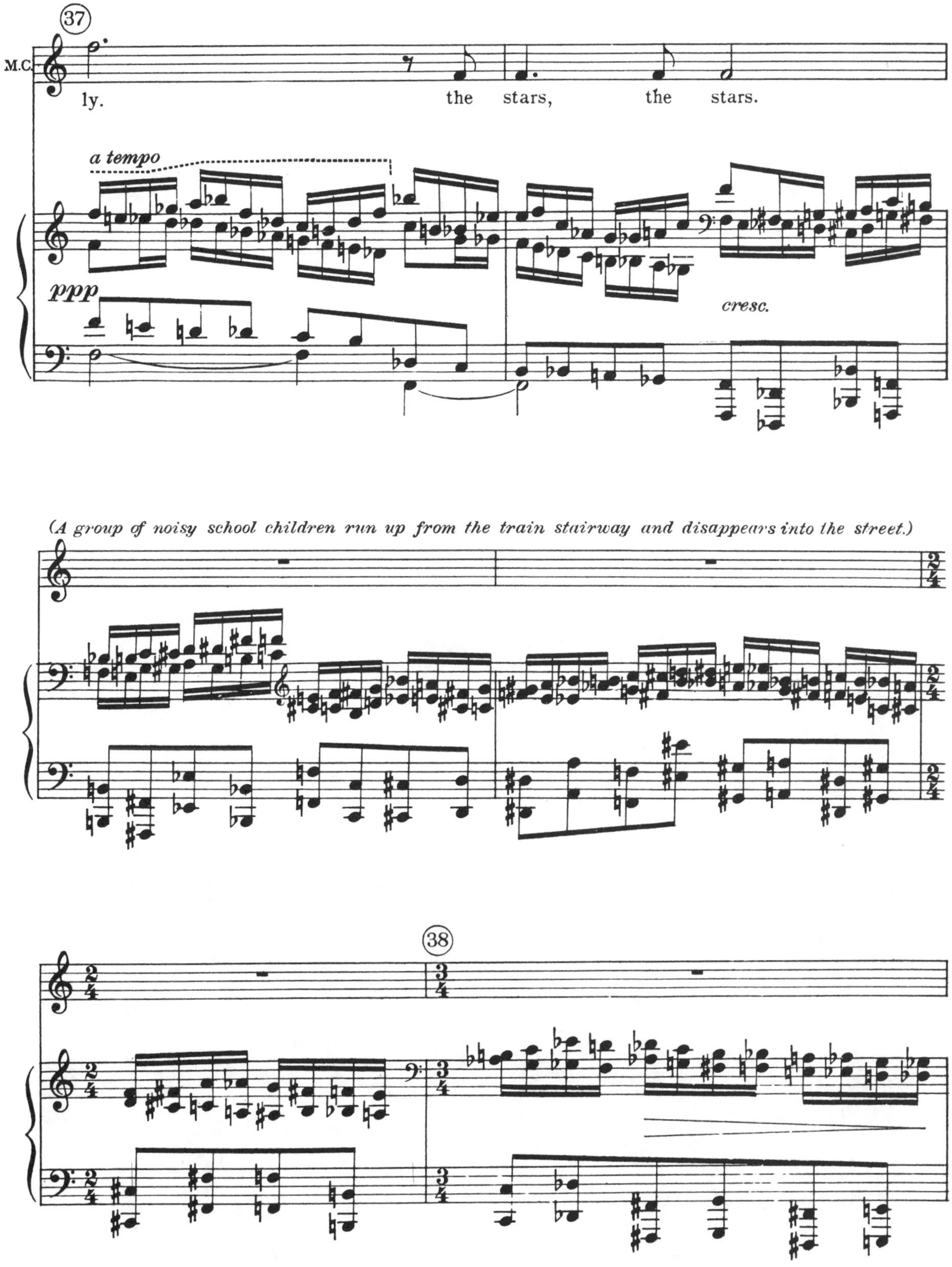

(A group of noisy school children run up from the train stairway and disappears into the street.)

38

mf
p
(Annina walks up to Michele)
rall.
pp
ppp
39
Annina
Ann.
Ev - 'ry - thing has changed and noth - ing
Michele
Mich.
pp espr.

Ann.
chang - es. I still must go my way and our
Mich.

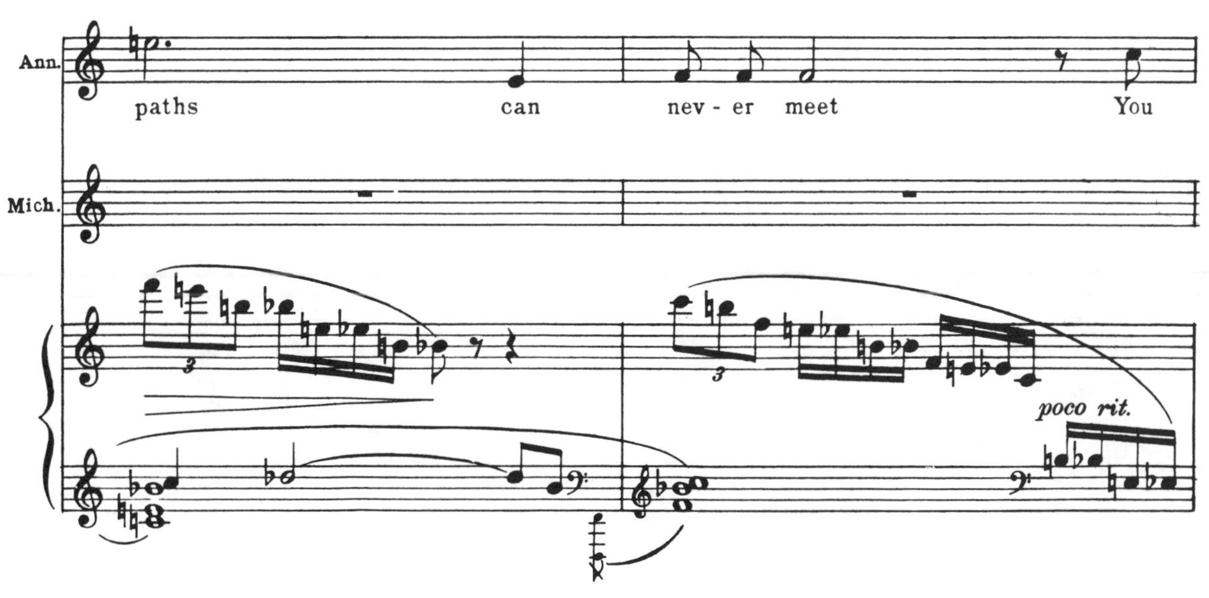
Ann.
paths can nev - er meet You
Mich.
poco rit.

poco rit.
40
a tempo
Ann.
know how dear you are to me.
hab dich im - mer lieb ge - habt.
Mich
On - ly you are left to me, An -
Ich hab nur noch dich al - lein. An -
pp
più mosso
poco rit.
a tempo
Ann
For you a - lone I stayed be -
Nur dei - net - we - gen blieb ich
Mich
ni - na, you, my sis - ter, you, my gen - tle
ni - na, mei - ne Schwes - ter, du, mein einz - ges
Ann
hind.
hier.
Now let me
Lass mich jetzt zu
Mich.
guid - ing light.
Le - bens - licht.
Noth - ing is
Al - les wird

41
Ann.
hast - en to my Love
Ah, Mi-
Mich.
lost if you re - main
ff
Ann.
che - le, don't you un-der-stand? I can no long-er help you.
Mich
42
Un poco più mosso
Ann.
Mich.
Why do you say that? An-ni - na.... You don't be-lieve what De-si -
Un poco più mosso
p
pp

Ann.
Oh, no, not that!
Mich.
de - ria said?
Why, then, do you say you can-not
f
p
Ann
Oh, yes, I can pray for you.
Mich.
help me an-y-more?
It's more than your prayers I
p
43
Ann.
His voice keeps calling me
How can one re - sist the voice of God?
Mich.
need.
It is my voice you hear.
mp

44
Ann.
On - ly by serv-ing Him.
Nur wer Ihm die-nen will.
Mich
Are-n't we all God's sons?
Sind wir nicht al-le Got-tes Kin-der?
Must-n't we all be
Wer-den nicht al - le ge -
f cresc.
p
Ann.
I can hope to save you, Mi-che - le.
Ich will dich zu ret - ten ver-su - chen.
Mich
saved?
ret - tet?
Is it in God's name
Gott wird dich nicht zwin gen,
ff

45
Ann.
My ev-er-last-ing wish is now my last de-sire.
Was ich mir im-mer wünsch-te, ist jetzt mein letz - ter Wunsch.
Mich.
that you for-sake your broth-er?
dei-nen Bru-der zu ver - las-sen.
8
ff
46
Andante
It's no use, Mi-che - le. I've made
Es ist zweck-los, Mi-che - le. Ich bin
I beg you, An-ni - na, you're still so young!
Ich bitt dich, An-ni - na, du bist so jung!
Andante
ppp
pppp
47
up my mind and not e-ven you can change it.
fest ent-schlos-sen, und du kannst nichts mehr än - dern.
(desperately)
Oh, please, An-
Bit - te, An-
ff

Ann
Mich.
This is good-bye, Mi-che-le.
Jetzt heisst es Ab-schied neh-men,
ni - na, do not a - ban - don me
ni - na, ver-lass mich jetzt noch nicht.
Good-bye for - ev - er.
Ab - schied für im - mer.
(with a cry)
(con un grido)
No!
Nein!
Go, then, your
Geh dei - ner
48
way, but you will car - ry with you my guilt and be
We - ge, doch ich be - las - te dich mit mei-ner Schuld, und ver-

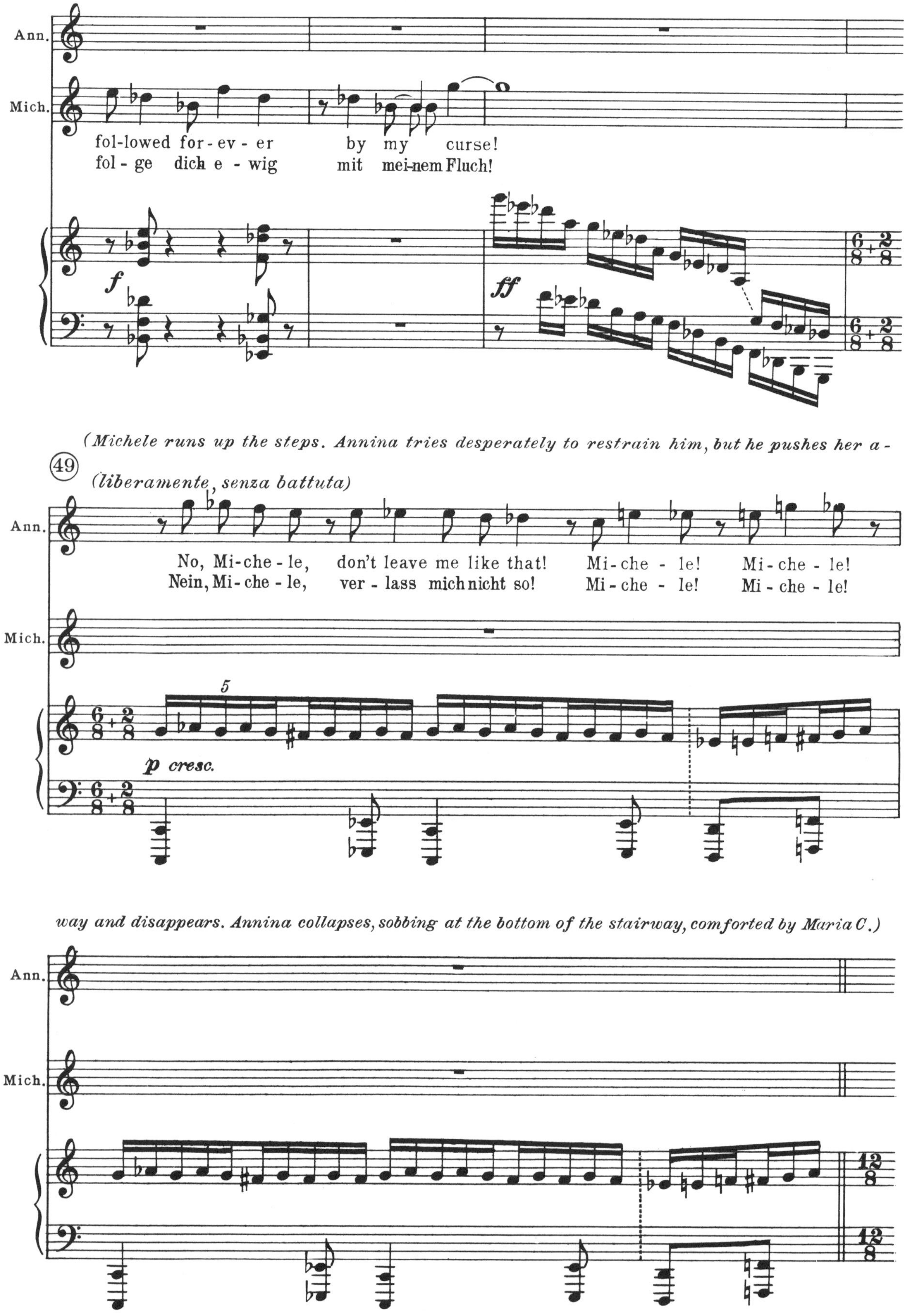

Ann.

Mich.

fol-lowed for-ev-er by my curse!
fol-ge dich e-wig mit mei-nem Fluch!

f *ff*

(Michele runs up the steps. Annina tries desperately to restrain him, but he pushes her a-

49 *(liberamente, senza battuta)*

Ann.

No, Mi-che-le, don't leave me like that! Mi-che-le! Mi-che-le!
Nein, Mi-che-le, ver-lass mich nicht so! Mi-che-le! Mi-che-le!

Mich.

p cresc.

f
ff
50
ff

51

dim.
p
ppp

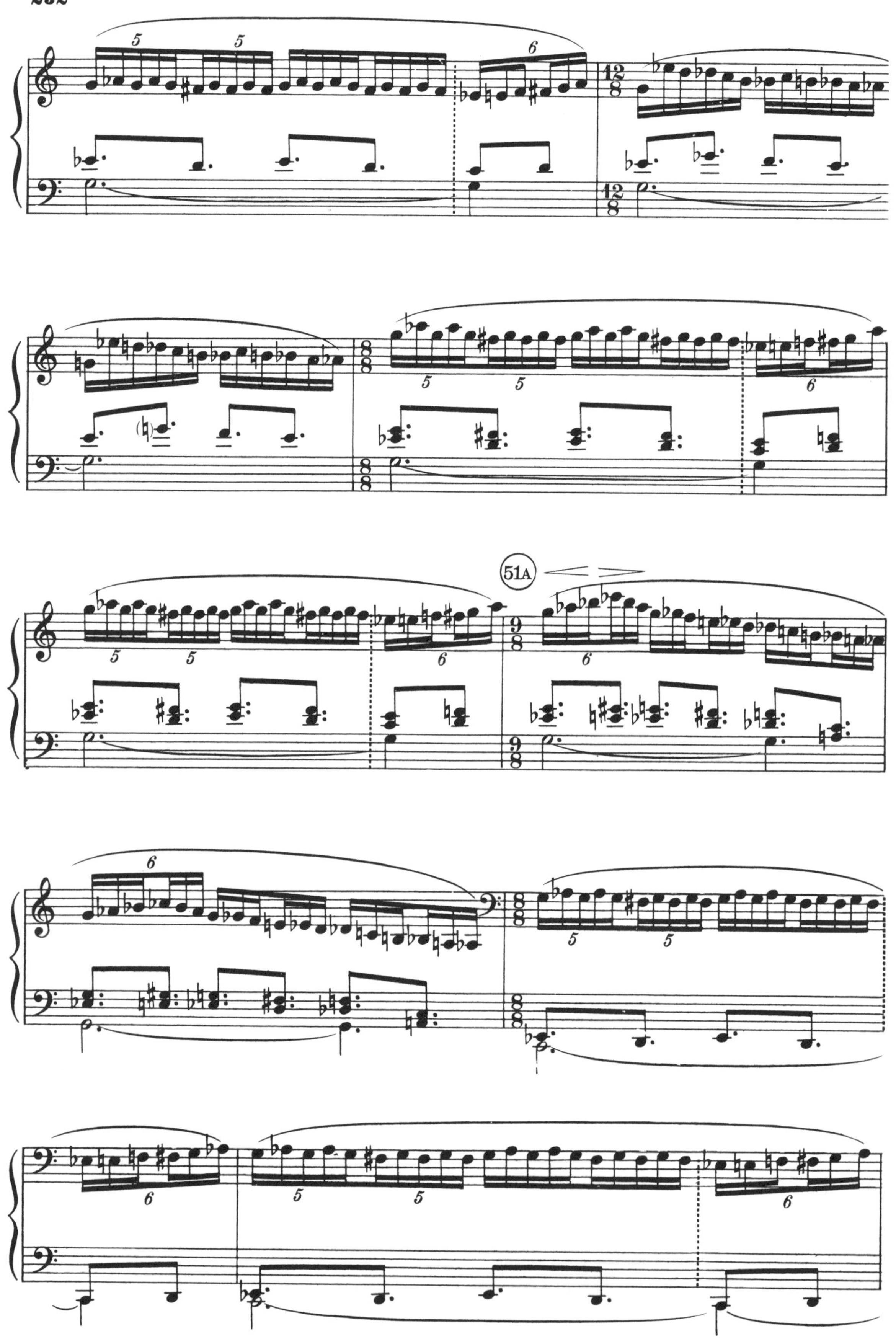
51A

51B
f
51C
ff

mf
p
5
6
51D
pppp
tr
(continuare ad lib.)
morendo

51E
Adagio ma non troppo
espr.
pp
poco rall.
3
51F
a tempo
poco rit.
a tempo
poco rit.
8
3
ff
8
poco rit.
a tempo
mf espr.

52
Andante mosso
f
53
pp dolce
espress.
mf
54
p
pp

55
p
poco più f
mf
p
mf
56
l.h.
ppp
p espress.
l.h.
57
(Curtain goes up)
mf
mf

Scene 2

(Annina's room, late afternoon. Annina, wrapped in an old shawl, lies back in her armchair, her eyes closed, her face extremely pale. A nun is sitting next to her. Don Marco is standing by the front door, as if anxiously waiting for someone. Carmela, who evidently had been crying, is sitting in a corner of the room, being comforted by Salvatore. ***In another corner of the room, a small group of women, among them Maria Corona with her son and Assunta, are kneeling in prayer.)***

A'ta
A - gnus Dei, qui tol - lis pec-ca-ta mun - di.
Do-mi-ne.
Mi-se-re-re no - bis.
4
4

A'ta
Chri-ste au-di-nos,
Chri-ste ex-au-di-nos.
A - men.
ppp
(parlato)
(spoken)
Chri - ste au-di-nos,
Chri - ste ex-au-di-nos.
A - men.
ppp
(parlato)
(spoken)
pp

59
Annina
Ann.
(opens her eyes)
Car - me - la?
Car - me - la!
Carmela
Car.
(running to her)
Yes, An-ni-na.
Ja, An-ni-na.
p molto espr.
p
(The nun silently tiptoes away, giving up her chair to Carmela.)
An-y news?
Et was Neues?
Not yet. We are all wait-ing and
Noch nicht. Wir al-le war-ten und
pp
60
Allegro moderato
(almost crying)
And still my voi - ces have told me,
A - ber... mei-ne Stim - men sag-ten doch...
pray-ing for you.
be - ten für-dich.
Allegro moderato
p

(far away)
(She closes her eyes,
Ann.
My voi - ces have told me.....
Mei-ne Stim - men sa - gen....
Car.
ppp
poco rall.
61
as if lost in a dream.)
(She opens her eyes.)
That I would take the veil to - day
Das ich den Schlei-er heu - te nehm...
What, An - ni - na?
Was, An - ni - na?
Andante
ppp
(liberamente)
I'm sure you will, An-ni - na. How could the church re-fuse what God de-sires?
Ja, ganz be-stimmt, An-ni - na. Wie kann die Kir-che ver-wei-gern, was Gott be-stimmt?

62
Allegro moderato
Ann.
Oh, I'm so a - fraid, Car-me - la, that I won't live un-til to -
Ach, ichhab so Angst, Car-me - la, dass ich den A-bend nicht er -
Car
Allegro moderato
pp
p
poco rall.
night
le - be.
(liberamente)
Why do you say that? You heard what the doc-tor said, that your
Wie kommst du dar - auf? Du weisst, was der Dok-tor sagt... das dein
3
63
Adagio
What lit-tle strength I have,
Das klei-ne biss-chen Kraft
heart is much strong-er to-day
Herz wie-der kräf - ti-ger ist.
Adagio
pp

64

Allegro moderato

(She leans back, her eyes closed.)

Ann. sweet, pa-tient Death has kind-ly lent me
hat mir der Tod für heut ge-lie-hen.

Car.

Allegro moderato

ppp

p cresc.

(suddenly, with great anxiety) *(liberamente)*

Ann. Car-me-la, Car-
Car-me-la, Car-

Car.

mf cresc.

Ann. me-la! Oh, here you are. I was just
me-la! Ach, da bist du ja... Ich ü-ber-

Car. What is it, An-ni-na?
Was hast du, An-ni-na?

pp

Ann.
think-ing if the per-mis-sion comes to-day, I have no white dress to
le - ge.... wenn die Er-laub-nis heu - te kommt, dann hab ich kein weiss - es
Car.
65
Andante
wear.
Kleid.
Don't wor-ry a-bout that, sil-ly girl. I have a sur-prise for you. Close your eyes.
Mach du dir kei-ne Sor-gen um dein Kleid. Du wirst ü-ber-rascht sein. Schau mal weg!
Andante
p dolce
A sur-prise, a sur-prise....
U-ber-rasch-en... willst du mich?
66
Allegro
(Carmela goes to a closet
Allegro
pp col ped.

where her wedding dress is hanging, takes it out and brings it over to Annina.)

Ann
mem - ber it. There is no gown in all the world I'd rath-er
wie - der. Ich weiss kein Kleid auf die-ser Welt, das mir heut
f espr.
69
wear to-day. Thank you. Leave it near me where I can look at it.
lie - ber wär. Dan - ke. Leg es hier-her, wo ich es seh-en kann.
poco rall.
pp a tempo
(Carmela lays the dress on the chair next to Annina.)
70
Allegro
ppp
p agitato

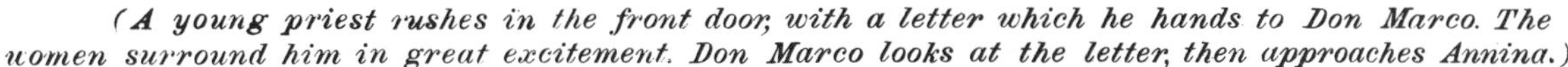

(A young priest rushes in the front door, with a letter which he hands to Don Marco. The women surround him in great excitement. Don Marco looks at the letter, then approaches Annina.)

mf cresc.

cresc.

(71)

Don Marco

D.M.

An-ni-na, An - ni - na, pre-pare your-
An-ni-na, An - ni - na, ich hab ei-ne

D.M.

self for a great joy The Church has grant-ed you your
freu - di - ge Nach-richt. Die Kir - che hat dei-nen Wunch er -

72
Annina
Andante, ma molto mosso
Ann.
Ah, I
Ach, wie
Carmela
Car.
D.M
wish
füllt,
Andante, ma molto mosso
Ann
knew
schön.
My voi - ces have told me
Ich weiss von mei-nen Stim - men,
(embracing her)
Car.
I'm so glad for you.
O, wie schön fur dich!
My An-ni - na!
Lieb-ste Freun-din!
D.M.

73
Ann.
Car.
D.M.
that I shall die to - night....
dass ich heut ster - ben muss...
but I shall die a
a - ber ich ster - be als
Je - sus will not for - sake His joy - ful
Je - sus er - war - tet sei - ne hol - de
poco accel.
rall.
bride.
Braut.
bride.
Braut.
(She leans back in her chair, breathing heavily, one hand over her heart.)
(liberamente)
I must rest a-while. Get read-y, Don Mar-co,
Ich bin gleich so-weit. Rich-tet schon al - les
p
pp

Ann.
I'll soon be all right
Lasst mich et-was ruhn.
Car-me-la, leave me a-lone for a
Car-me-la, bit-te, ver-las-semich
Car.
D.M.
Yes, rest a-while
Ja, ru-heeinwenig.
pp
74
Ann.
while. I want to pray.
jetzt. Ich möch-te be-ten.
Car.
Yes, An-ni-na.
Ja, An-ni-na.
(Don Marco motions to the women to leave the room.)
DM.
Keep them out for a
War-tet draus-sen so
Allegretto
p
(The women crowd outside the door, which is guarded by Carmela. Don Marco kneels in front of the little altar.)
D.M.
while.
lang.
poco sf
pp

75
Annina
Lento
Ann.
Oh, my Love, at last the hour has come.
Oh, mein Gott, nun ist die Stun - de da.
pp
Help me now to bear so great a joy. Hold
Stär - ke mich für dies-es Freu - den fest. Ver-
76
back, O Death, for still a lit-tle while, then kind - ly
schon mich, Tod, noch ei - nen Au-gen blick, dann komm zu
rall.
a tempo
p

77
Ann.
come and make the night e - ter - nal for His e - ter - nal
mir, und lass-es e - wig Nacht sein für Sei - ne e - wige

78
(with sudden anxiety)
Ann.
love. Sus-tain me, O God. Car-me-la,
Lie - be. O hilf mir, mein Gott. Car-me-la,
poco rall.
p poco agitato

(Carmela comes over to her.)
Ann.
where is the bri-dal veil? Where is my
wo ist der Schlei - er? Wo ist mein

Ann.
crown?
Kranz?
Carmela
Car.
Ev-'ry-thing is read-y. We are wait-ing for you.
Al-les ist be-reit. Und wir war-ten auf dich.
ppp
79
Andante
Yes, Car-me-la,
Ja, Car-me-la,
(liberamente)
(putting one arm around her shoulders)
Come on. Try to get up. I'm pray-ing for you.
Steh auf. Ver-su-che es nur.... Ich be-te für dich.
Andante
p
poco rit.
pray for me. I'm a-fraid, Car-me-la. I may
bet für mich, dass ich die gros-se Freu-de er-

a tempo
Ann.
faint for joy. Feel how faint and wild is my heart.
tra - gen kann. Fühl nur, wie mein Herz hef - tig schlägt.

80
f
(with great intensity)
Ann.
I have so lit-tle strength left. Hold back, O
Bald hört es auf, zu schla - gen. Ver - schon mich,
ppp

rall.
Ann.
Death, for still a lit - tle while, then
Tod, noch ei - nen Au - gen - blick, dann
rall.

81
Lento
Ann.
come at last and
end - - lich komm, und

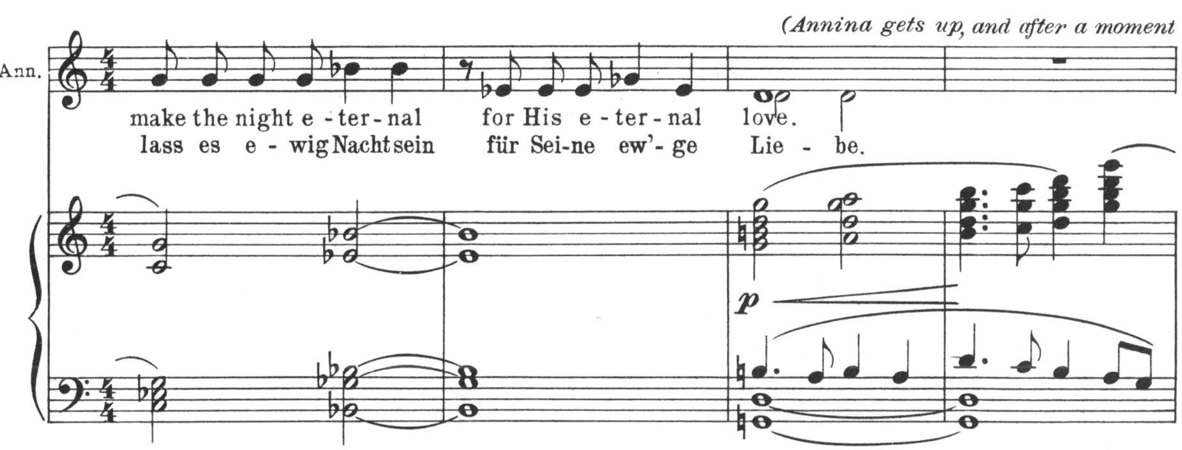
(Annina gets up, and after a moment
Ann.
make the night e - ter - nal for His e - ter - nal love.
lass es e - wig Nacht sein für Sei - ne ew'- ge Lie - be.

of hesitation, leaning on Carmela's arm, she walks slowly into her room. The nun follows them, carrying the white dress.)
Ann.
rall.

(82)

(During the following scene, Don Marco, helped by the young priest, clothes himself in preparation for the ceremony. In the meantime, neighbors crowd into the room, most of the women carrying lighted candles.)

Assunta

Allegro vivo

Maria C.
M.C.
A'ta
83
Oh, —
O die
dy - ing, and wants to stop — her from tak-ing the veil. —
Schlei-er nimmt; er ist sonst im Stan - de und kommt noch hier-her. —
poor girl.
Ärm - ste!
He does-n't care if she lives or she es. He does-n't care. All that he
Es ist ihm gleich, ob sie lebt od - er stirbt. Ihm ist es gleich, wenn er sie
84
cares is to drag her to hell right af - ter him.
nur in die fin - ster - ste Höl - le mit - neh - men kann.

Maria C.
pp
M.C.
Just think,
just think,
Assunta
pp
A'ta
Just think,
just think,
Mein Gott,
mein Gott,
Sal.
pp
Sal.
Just think,
just think,
ppp
M.C.
what that poor girl had to suf-fer be-cause of Mi - che - le.
A'ta
what that poor girl had to suf-fer be-cause of Mi - che - le.
was muss die Ar-me doch we-gen Mi-che-le er - dul - den
Sal.
what that poor girl had to suf-fer be-cause of Mi - che - le.

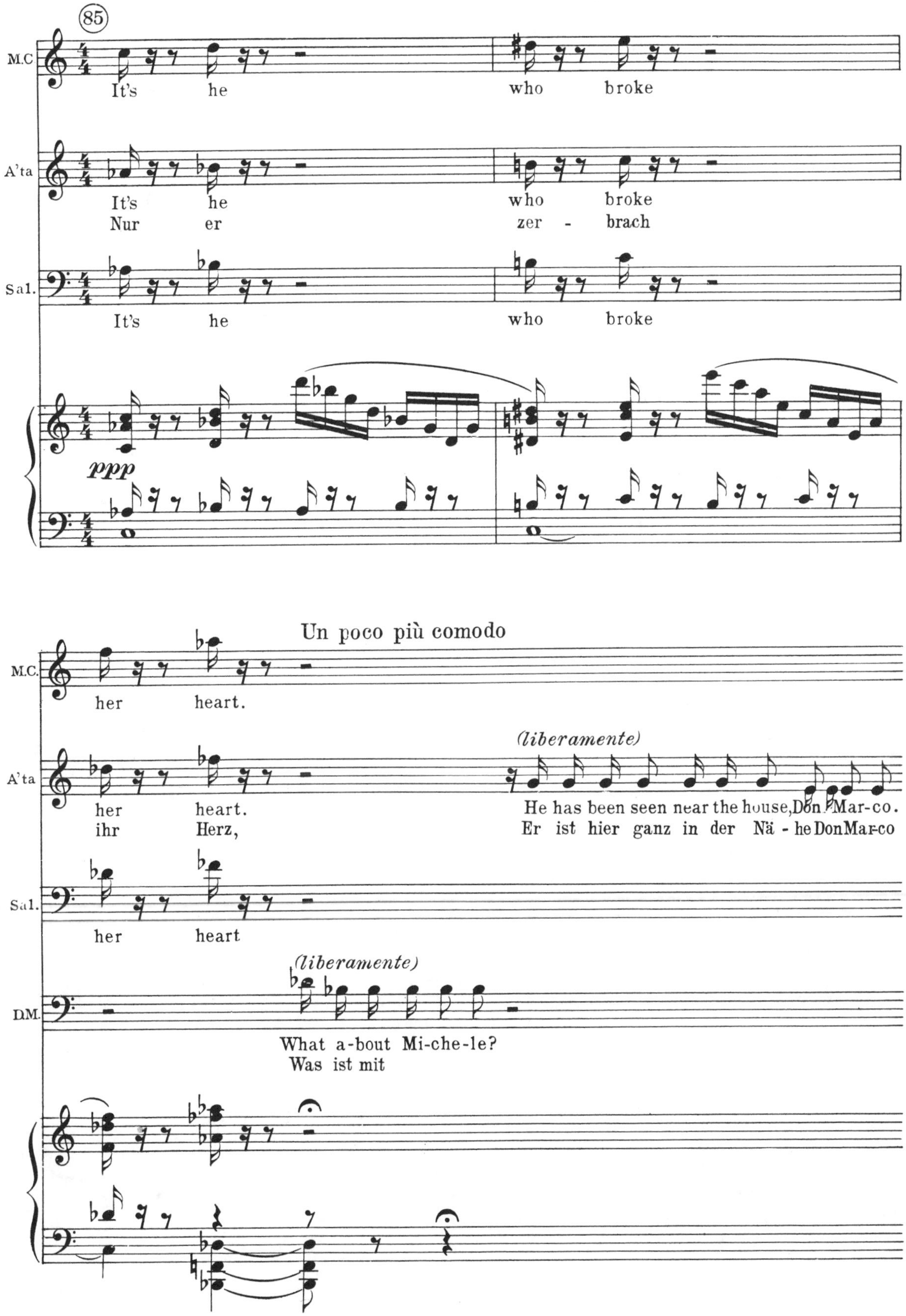

Un poco più comodo

M.C.
her heart.

(liberamente)

A'ta
her heart. He has been seen near the house, Don Mar-co.
ihr Herz, Er ist hier ganz in der Nä - he Don Mar-co

Sal.
her heart

(liberamente)

D.M.
What a-bout Mi-che-le?
Was ist mit

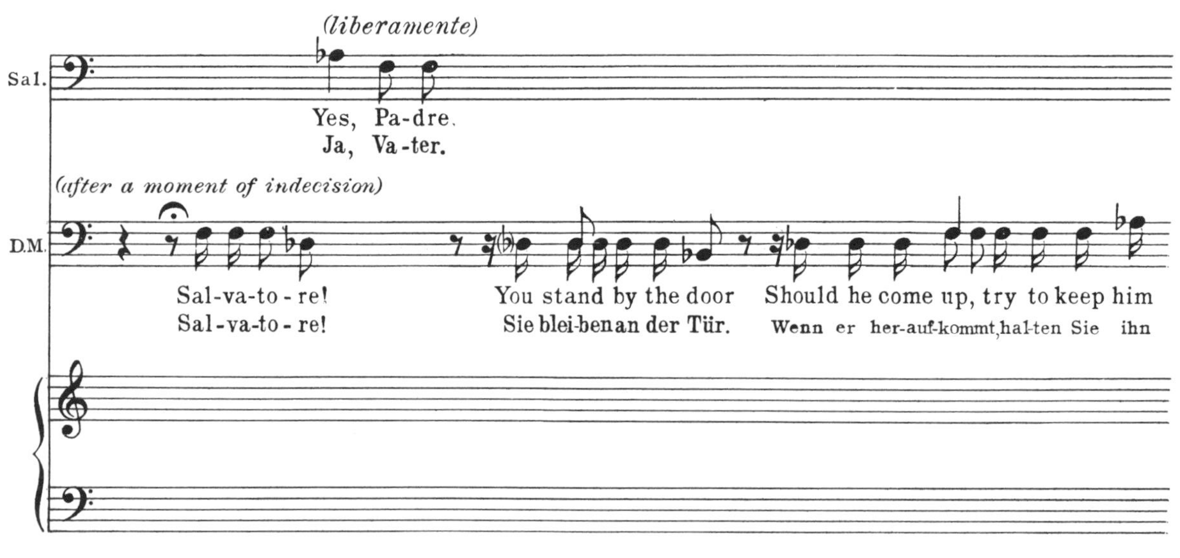
(liberamente)
Sal.
Yes, Pa-dre.
Ja, Va-ter.
(after a moment of indecision)
D.M.
Sal-va-to-re!
Sal-va-to-re!
You stand by the door
Sie blei-ben an der Tür.
Should he come up, try to keep him
Wenn er her-auf-kommt, hal-ten Sie ihn

Sal.
Should-n't we call the po-lice?
Soll'n wir nicht die Po - li - zei ru-fen?
D.M.
out.
fest.
No, not yet.
Nein, noch nicht.
We must think of her now.
Das möcht ich ver-mei - den.

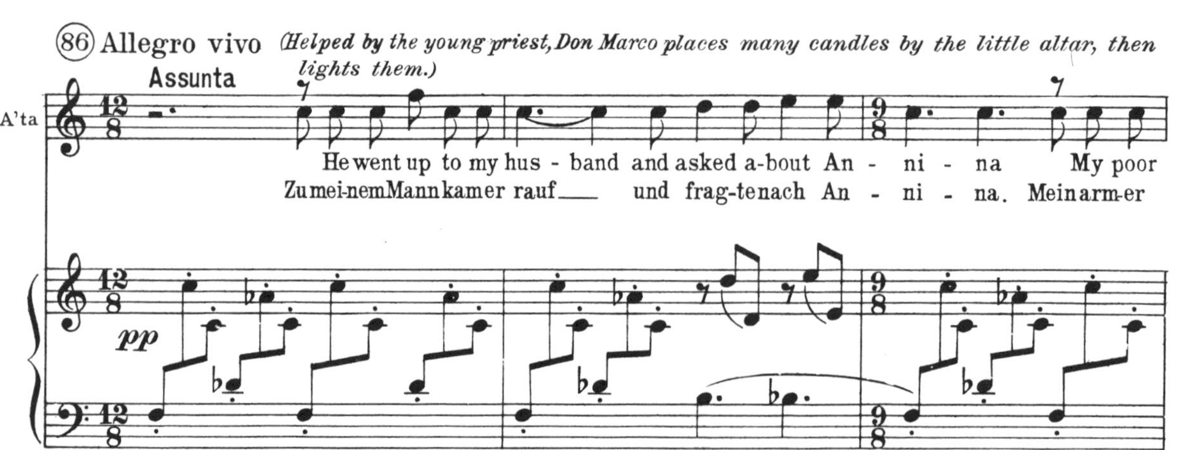
86 Allegro vivo
(Helped by the young priest, Don Marco places many candles by the little altar, then lights them.)
Assunta
A'ta
He went up to my hus - band and asked a-bout An - ni - na My poor
Zu mei-nem Mann kam er rauf und frag-te nach An - ni - na. Mein arm-er
pp

A'ta
hus-band kept talk-ing and talk-ing and hop - ing that some-one there
Mann hat ge - re - det wie'n Buch weil er hoff - te, dass in der Zeit
Maria C.
M.C.
87
Oh, poor girl!
Oh, die Ärm - ste!
A'ta
would go call the po- lice.
je-mand die Po-li - zei ruft.
Sal.
Sal.
Oh poor girl!
Oh, die Ärm - ste!
p
pp
M.C.
It is be-cause of his sins that she's dy - ing, dy - ing.
Weil er ein Mör-der ist, muss sie so jung schon ster - ben.
A'ta
He is the cross she has to bear un-til the end.
Er ist das Kreuz, das sie zu tra-gen hat bis zum Tod.
Sal.

88
One tenor
pp
Ten.
Just think,
Mein Gott,
just think,
mein Gott,
pp
Sal
Just think,
just think,
One bass
pp
Bass
Just think,
just think,
8
ppp
Ten.
what the poor girl had to suf-fer be-cause of Mi - che - le.
was muss die Ar-me nur we-gen Mi-che - le er - dul - den.
Sal.
what the poor girl had to suf-fer be-cause of Mi - che - le.
Bass
what the poor girl had to suf-fer be-cause of Mi - che - le.
tr

89
(Salvatore goes to stand guard at the front door.)
Carmela
Car.
An - ni - na is read - y.
An - ni - na ist be - reit.
Don Marco
D.M.
Let us be-gin.
Fan-gen wir an!
90
Maestoso
(Dressed as a bride, her loose hair covered by a white veil, Annina appears in the doorway
SOP.
Glo - ria ti - bi Do - mi - ne in sae - cu - lum et in sae - cu - lum
ALTO
TENOR
Glo - ria ti - bi Do - mi - ne in sae - cu - lum et in sae - cu - lum
BASS.

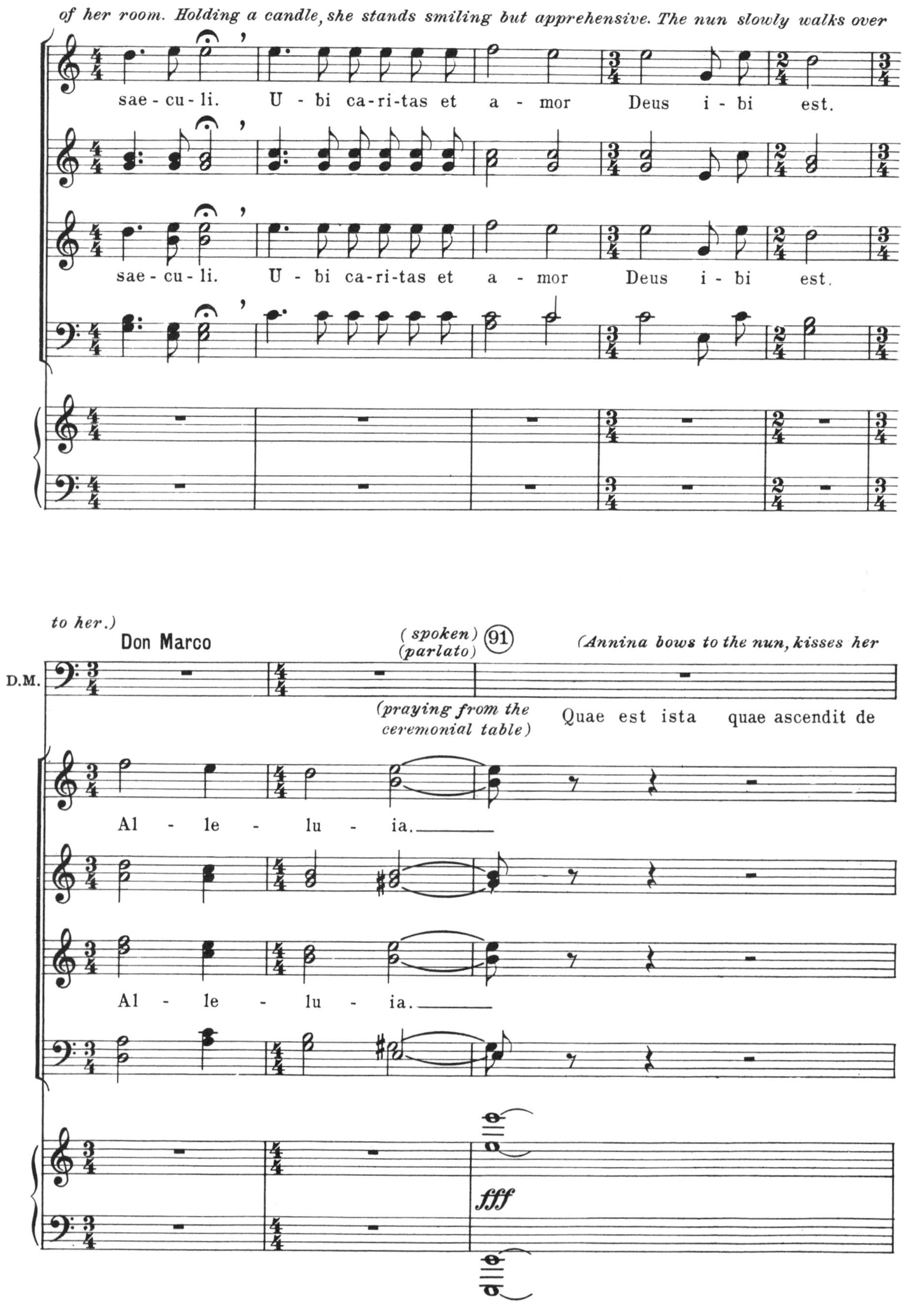

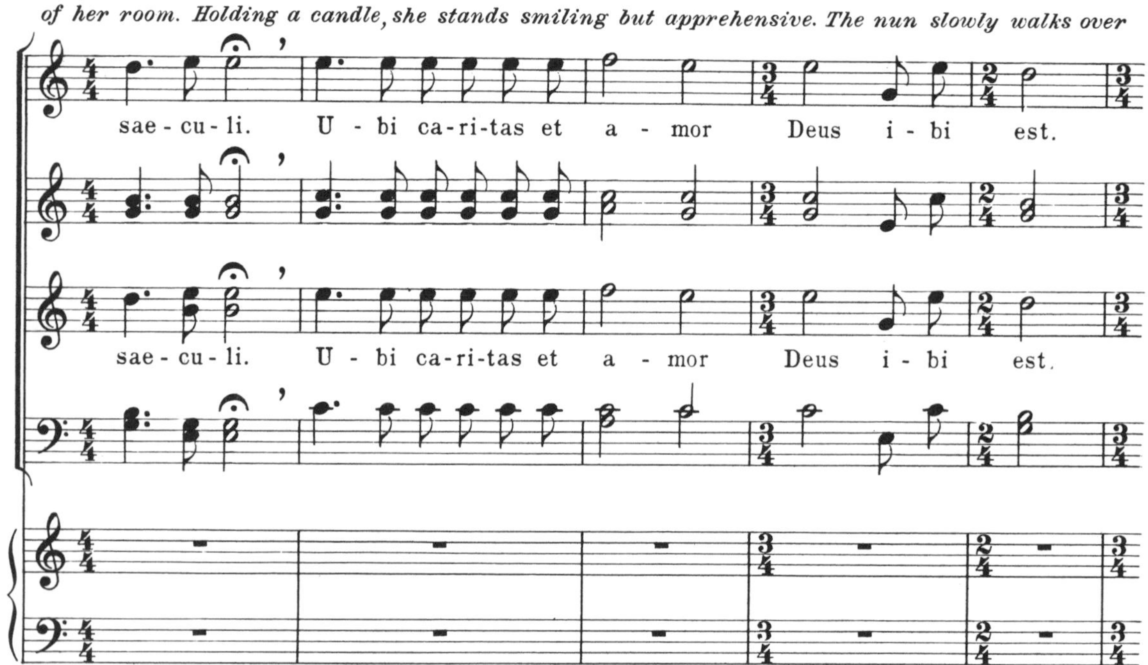

to her.)

Don Marco

(spoken) 91 *(Annina bows to the nun, kisses her*

(parlato)

D.M.

(praying from the ceremonial table) Quae est ista quae ascendit de

Al - le - lu - ia.

Al - le - lu - ia.

fff

Andante
hand, and is led across the stage to a screen which has been placed in a corner of the room. She
D.M.
deserto, deliciis affluens, innixa super dilectuum suum? Tota pulchra es amica mea
SOPRANO
ALTO I
p
Ky - ri - e e - le - i - son. Ky -
ALTO II
p
Ky - ri - e e -
TENOR
BASS
92
steps behind the screen, still visible to the audience.)
D.M.
suavis et decora; veni de Libano; sponsa mea; veni de Libano, veni coronaberis.
Ky - ri - e, Ky - ri - e e - le -
- ri - e, Ky - ri - e e - le - i -
le - i - son. Ky - ri - e e - le -
Ky - ri -
mf
pp

- i - son. Ky - ri-e e - le - i - son.
son. Ky-ri - e e - le - i - son, e-le -
- i-son. Ky-ri - e, Ky - ri - e e-le-i-son.
Ky - ri-e e -
e, Ky - ri - e e-le - i - son, e -
p
93
f
Chri - ste e - le-i -
- i - son. Chri - ste e - le-i -
Chri - ste e - le-i -
le - i - son.
le - - i - son.
pp
f col ped.
8

son. Chri - ste e - le -
son. Chri - ste e - le - i -
son. Chri - ste e - le -
ff
Chri - ste e - le -
BASS I
ff
Chri - ste e - le - i -
BASS II
ff
Chri - ste e - le -
i - son.
94
p subito (senza accellerando)
Al - le - lu - ia,
- son. Al - le - lu - ia,
p subito
i - son. Al - le - lu - ia,
p subito
i - son. Al - le - lu - ia,
- son. Al - le - lu - ia,
p subito
i - son. Al - le - lu - ia,
pp subito

più f
Al - le - lu - ia, Al - le - lu - ia,
Al - le - lu - ia, Al - le - lu - ia,
più f
Solo
Al - le - lu - ia, Al - le - lu - ia,
più f
Al - le - lu - ia, Al - le - lu - ia,
(pp)
f
ff
Al - le - lu - ia, Al - le - lu - ia, Al -
ff
Al - le - lu - ia, Al - le - lu - ia, Al -
ff
ff
Al - le - lu - ia, Al - le - lu - ia, Al -
ff
Al - le - lu - ia, Al - le - lu - ia, Al -
ff
ff

(Annina knocks twice against the screen. It is opened by the nun who takes the candle from her and hands it to someone near by.)
Annina
le - lu - ia.
le - lu - ia.
le - lu - ia.
le - lu - ia.
lunga
lunga
95
Andante moderato ma con moto
Ann.
(still standing by the screen)
The Mer - cy of God and the
Die Gna - de Got-tes und das
Don Marco
D.M.
What do you ask, my daugh - ter?
Was ist dein Be - geh - ren?
Andante moderato ma con moto
pp

Ann
ho - ly hab - it of re - lig - ion
heil'-ge Kleid_ uns-rer Kir - che.
D.M
Do you ask this of your own free
Und dies be - gehrst du aus frei - em
96
Ann.
It is my will and my de-sire.
Es ist mein Wil - le und mein Wunsch.
D.M.
will?
Wil-len?
Do you re-nounce
Und wi-der sagst du
Ann
Yes, I do.
Ich wi-der sa-ge.
D.M.
Sa - tan?
Sa - tan?
And all his works and
All sei-nem Werk und sei-ner

97
Ann.
Yes, I do.
Ich wi - der sa - ge.
D.M.
all his pomps? ___
eit - len Pracht. ___
Con-firm, O
Be - fest' - ge, o
Ann.
D.M.
God, what You have wrought in her.
Gott, was Du in ihr ge - wir - ket hast.
En - ter,
Tritt nun
98
D.M.
there-fore the tem-ple of the Lord, that you may be -
ein in das Hei - lig - tum des Herrn, auf dass der - einst du
f

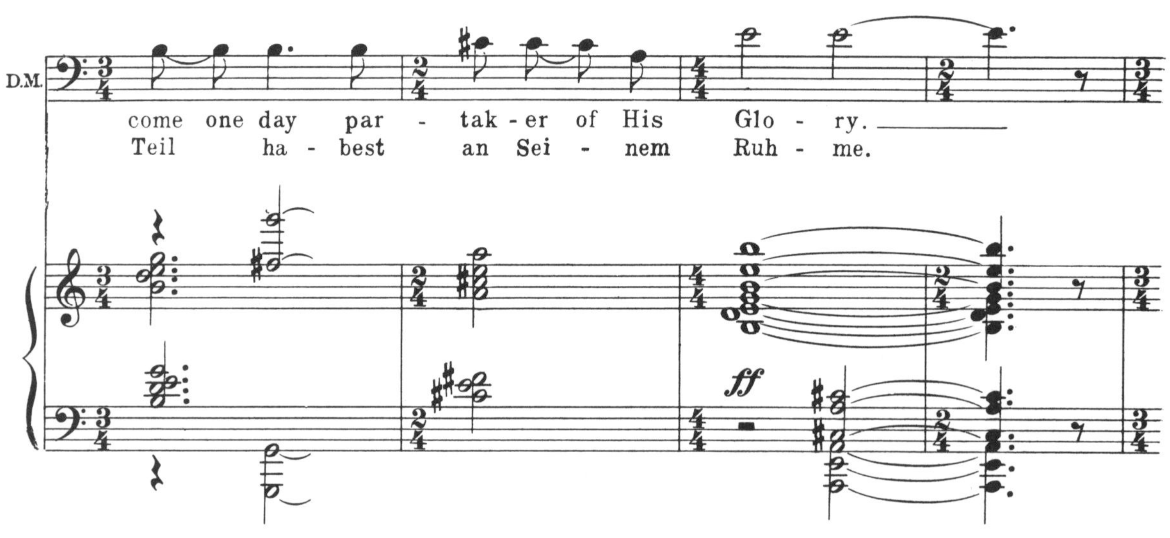
D.M.
come one day par - tak - er of His Glo - ry.
Teil ha - best an Sei - nem Ruh - me.
ff

Chorus
SOPS.
(The nun leads Annina to the center of the room and has her kneel; then removes the wreath of blossoms.)
legatissimo
pp
Ve - ni, spon - sa Chri - sti, ac - ci - pe co - ro - nam quam ti - bi
ALTOS
legatissimo
pp

99
(Annina prostrates herself
Do - mi - nus pre - pa - ra - bit in ae - ter - num.
mf

on the bare floor. Her extended arms form a cross. The nun covers her with a black cloth.)

D.M.
grand-eur of this earth, a-rise, my child, and be re-born in Christ, our
Grös-se die-ser Er-de. Steh auf, mein Kind, sei neu ge-bo-ren in Chri - sto, dem
100 Allegro
D.M.
Lord.
Herrn.
SOPRANO I
pp
Ah
SOPRANO II
pp
Ec - ce quam bo - num et
ALTO I
pp
Ec - ce quam bo - num et
ALTO II
pp
Ah
TENOR
pp
Ec - ce quam bo - num et
BASS
Allegro
p

Ah
quam jucundum, ecce quam bonum et
quam jucundum, ecce quam bonum et
Ah
quam jucundum, ecce quam bonum et
Ah
quam jucundum, habitare fratres in
quam jucundum, habitare fratres in
Ah
quam jucundum, habitare fratres in

101
(The nun approaches, Annina removes the black cloth and helps her to her knees. At this very moment Michele bursts into the room, but
Ah
u - - num. Ec - ce quam bo - num et quam ju - cun - dum,
u - - num. Ec - ce quam bo - num et quam ju - cun - dum,
Ah
u - - num. Ec - ce quam bo - num et quam ju - cun - dum,

is immediately grabbed and restrained by Salvatore and another man. Everybody turns

Ah.

ec - ce quam bo - num et quam.

ec - ce quam bo...

Ah.

ec - ce quam.

Presto

ff

toward Michele except Annina who, completely transfixed, keeps staring at the holy image

on the altar.)
Michele
Mich.
103
An - ni - na, An - ni - na!
ff
ff
Salvatore
Sal.
(liberamente)
(in a whisper)
If you go near her I'll kill you.
Wenn du dich ihr nä - herst, bring ich dich um.
104
Molto moderato
Michele
Listen, An - ni - na!
Hö - re, An - ni - na!
pp
Lis - ten to me! Why leave the world al -
Ein - mal_ noch! Die Welt wird öd und leer,

Mich.
ready - y so be - reft of love? Con - sid - er, An - ni - na,
wenn du sie ver - las - sen willst. Be - sinn dich, An - ni - na,
poco sf
Mich.
you're still in time Why seek for God's face in a cloud - ed
noch ist es Zeit. Was suchst du Lie - be in der Nä - he
cresc. poco a poco
105
Mich.
mir - ror when you can find it burn - ing in your broth - er's heart!
Got - tes, sie brennt für dich viel heis - ser in dei - nes Bru - ders Herz!
f
pp cresc.
Mich.
Look at me, An - ni - na! Come to your sens - es! It is there
Sieh mich an, An - ni - na! Komm wie - der zu dir! Wo ein Mensch
ff
pp

Mich.
where hu-man mis-er-y is great-est that God shines
in sei-ner höch-sten Not ist, ist Gott am
cresc.
106
most
näch - - sten.
I
Ich
f
need you, An-ni-na, my sis-ter
brauch dich, An-ni-na, mei-ne Schwe-ster!
I
Ich
ff
marcatissimo
need all the love you can give
brauch dei-ne Lie-be für mich,

107
(There is a long, tense silence. But Annina still remains motionless, as if nothing had happened and time had not passed.)
Don Marco
lunga
(liberamente)
D.M.
You are too late, Mi-che-le. She can no long-er hear you
Es ist zu spät, Mi-che-le. Sie kann dich nicht mehr hö-ren.
pp
108
(Don Marco signals to his acolyte to resume the cere-
Maria C.
M.C.
Sur - ge
Carmela
Car.
Sur - - ge a-mi-ca
Assunta
A'ta
Sur - - ge a-mi-ca
D.M.
Let her leave the world in peace.
Lass sie nun in Frie-den gehn.
pp

mony. He then approaches Annina, followed by the acolyte, who carries a pair of scissors

(Don Marco cuts Annina's

M.C. tran - si - it et re - ces - - sit.

Car. tran - si - it im - ber a - bi - it et re - ces - sit.

A'ta tran - si - it im - ber a - bi - it et re - ces - sit.

D.M. nounced all worldly van - i - ties.
sagt hast der ir - di - schen Ei - tel - keit.

110

hair and places it on the tray. Michele, who has been watching in silence, suddenly breaks into loud weeping.)

Chorus

SOPRANO
Ve - ni co - lum - ba me - a.

ALTO

TENOR
Ve - ni co - lum - ba me - a.

BASS

(Michele, having gained control of himself, stands staring at the remainder of the ceremony, stunned and incredulous.)

M.C.
Car.
A'ta
D.M.
— ad - ve - nit. Vox tur - tu - ris au -
— ad - ve - nit. Vox tur - tu - ris au -
— ad - ve - nit. Vox tur - tu - ris au -
ty, and may you walk in the way of hu - mil - i - ty and
heit, und wan - dle den Weg der De - mut und Wahr - haf - tig -
SOPRANOS
pp
Vox tur - tu - ris au -
ALTO
pp
di - ta est in ter - ra nos - tra.
di - ta est in ter - ra nos - tra.
di - ta est in ter - ra nos - tra.
(holding a ring in his hands)
truth. Re - ceive now, the ring of
keit. Em - pfan - ge nun den Ring des
unis
di - ta est in ter - ra nos - tra.

111
DM.
faith.
Glau - bens.
ppp SOPRANOS
Sur - ge a - mi - ca me - a, sur - ge co-lum-ba
ppp ALTOS
ppp TENORS
Sur - ge a - mi - ca me - a, sur - ge co-lum-ba
ppp BASSES
ppp
DM.
me - a. Ve - ni, ve - ni a - mi - ca
ff
me - a Ve - ni, ve - ni a - mi - ca

(Everyone kneels except Michele. Annina, at the end of her strength, sways slightly, as if making a desperate effort to move, but is unable to do so.)

Carmela

(anxiously)

Car. Go on, Annina.
Geh, Annina.

me - a.

me - a.

(112) *(Annina, very slowly, with apparent effort, takes a few steps toward Don Marco.*

p molto espr.

f

Then she suddenly sinks to the floor. Carmela, who has been anxiously watching her, quickly catches her as she collapses and kneels down holding Annina in her arms. No one moves except Don Marco who bends over Annina, lifts her lifeless arm and places the gold ring on her finger.)

pp subito